NAVIGATING LIFE'S TRANSITIONS

CONNECTING YOUR MEANS TO YOUR MEANING

Printed in the United States of America

First Edition: July 2014
10 9 8 7 6 5 4 3 2

Library of Congress Cataloging-in-Publication Data
Kadish, Joshua.
Navigating life's transitions: connecting your means to your meaning /
Joshua Kadish, Nicole V. Mayer.—1st ed. p. cm.
ISBN Paperback: 979-8-877238-76-3
Library of Congress Control Number: 2014943817

"No matter where you are in life, chances are there will be major transitions in your future. These transitions will most certainly involve your finances. If you're tired of feeling pressure from the financial industry to buy a product to solve your issues, you're not alone. In this book, you will learn from real-life scenarios that there are true holistic planners who will put your interests ahead of theirs. It's a different—and, in my opinion, better—approach and one that everyone deserves. Don't wait until the life transitions hit you to put your plan together. With the help of the right holistic advisor, you can experience less stress on both a personal and financial basis. This book will allow you to see what you should expect from a true financial advisor. Without proper knowledge, you could fall prey to the financial salesperson. Don't let that happen to you!"

Dean Barber, *America's Wealth Management Show* Host, Author

"Josh Kadish and I lead mission-driven firms. Peak Advisor Alliance's mission is: 'We enhance the lives of advisors and the families they serve through in-spiration, innovation, and implementation.' Josh, Nicole, and Allworth Financial help us fulfill our mission by delivering holistic financial planning to their clients."

Ron Carson, CFP®, ChFC®, CFS, *New York Times* bestseller and founder and CEO of Carson Wealth Management Group; #7 advisor in the U.S. as ranked by *Bar-ron's* magazine.

"Anyone going through some form of life transition should read this book! Josh and Nicole do a great job of making the complex seem simple and understandable. If you are trying to figure out if you are on the right course to achieving your long-term goals and dreams, this book is a great educational tool to help guide you in making future decisions with confidence."

Rick Law, Lead Attorney, Law Hesselbaum, LLP

This book is dedicated to those who find themselves at a turning point in their lives and recognize the need to become educated on their current course and future direction. We praise those who exercise the courage to navigate a path in life driven by their core values, a personal mission statement, and the passion to connect their means to their larger meaning as they attain *True Wealth*—all of the things money can't buy.

CONTENTS

ACKNOWLEDGMENTS

JOSH KADISH

My deepest gratitude goes to my parents and my grandmother for being true heroes and exemplary role models. I also want to acknowledge my wife for her unwavering love, support, and confidence, as well as my two sons, who inspire me every day to be the best father, friend, and person I can be. Words can't express how fortunate and blessed I feel to have you in my life.

NICOLE MAYER

Thank you to my parents for their continued guidance, love, support, and confidence. I also want to acknowledge my wonderful son, who motivates me to work continually to be a good mother and a role model to others. I am so grateful for the relationships and remarkable people who have crossed my path; they have helped shape my life.

INTRODUCTION

"Money. If only I had more of it, things would be better."

That's how many of us feel—until something happens in life that shakes us to our core . . . something that money alone can't fix. In those critical moments of vulnerability and anxiety, we pause and think about what is truly important. We wonder: how much of that government-printed green stuff do we really need to find "*True Wealth*"? How can we connect our wealth to our purpose to live a more enriched life? How can we make future career, personal, and financial decisions with confidence?

As you read this book, you may find yourself in some type of life transition, whether planned or unplanned. Perhaps you are approaching retirement and are unsure of what lifestyle you can you afford for the next third of your life. Perhaps the company you worked with for twenty years is downsizing, and you were recently called into a conference room for the conversation every professional dreads: the moment you are let go. Perhaps the relationship you thought would last a lifetime has crumbled, leaving you to reimagine a life without your longtime partner or the income he or she provided. Whatever transition you face, it is probably with fear and uncertainty. But it doesn't have to be that way.

Our names are Joshua Kadish and Nicole Mayer, and we have worked with people like you—people like *us*—over the course of three decades. We are Life Transition Specialists®.

Whenever we say that, newcomers give us a quizzical look. "What are Life Transition Specialists?" they ask. "We thought you were financial planners!"

We understand. What we offer and the way we offer it is unique, and this new type of service and relationship was borne out of frustration we both felt with the state of the financial industry.

1

At Allworth Financial we believe that the financial services model has been broken. We both entered the industry excited to advise people on ways to manage their money. Before very long, we each learned the reality of the industry: it wasn't designed to put clients and their specific needs first. We both believed a different way of helping people existed. A way that went beyond focusing on how much money was in the bank or what products to invest in. Our way is designed to help clients identify their true goals in life—knowing that their latest transition may have altered the goals they've had for years. Our next step is to thoroughly educate clients so they completely understand their financial picture and feel confident in making decisions going forward. Then, once our clients have a deeper understanding of their personal, professional, and life goals, we help them connect their finances—or their *means*—to support their newly defined *meaning*.

The result? Our clients gain a feeling of freedom and security that enables a new sense of purpose.

In this book, you'll get a good understanding of how and why we formed 2nd Opinion Partners now Allworth Financial and how our approach to wealth manage-ment is different. This will be helpful as you read about some of the typi-cal transitional situations our clients face. Whether through downsizing, divorce, death of a spouse, a sudden increase in wealth, illness, or the need for a second opinion, we guide our clients through the process with respect, empathy, professionalism, and a deep desire to do what is best for each individual's circumstance.

At the end of each client chapter, we'll provide some thinking points for you to consider for your own situation. However, before making any significant changes to your financial life, we strongly suggest that you contact us or another holistic planner who is held to a fiduciary standard (a high standard of care that requires clients' best interests be placed first). As you read these client-inspired, fictional stories and accompany our heroes on their journeys, consider this: what is *your* definition of *"True Wealth"*?

CHAPTER 1

LIFE LESSONS

"THAT'S THE THING ABOUT LESSONS, YOU ALWAYS LEARN
THEM WHEN YOU DON'T EXPECT THEM OR WANT THEM."

Cecelia Ahern, Novelist, *If You Could See Me Now*

Josh looked at the thick white phone book commanding the center of his small desk, which sat in a small cubicle inside a small office next to three other small cubicles. Each cubicle was outfitted with the most valuable tool available: the telephone. Josh shook his head as his boss's instructions echoed in his ears: "Just write the damn ticket!" Josh knew what that meant. He may have been new to the brokerage world, but he knew he was supposed to thumb through the phone book, pick a name, and cold call someone. Then he was supposed to convince that person to buy the mutual fund the brokerage was promoting and write the ticket for the order. It didn't matter how old the potential clients were, how much money they had, or whether the fund was the best for each person's situation. What was important—at least to Josh's boss—was making the sale. The sale and the consequent commission, that is.

This wasn't what Josh had envisioned when he'd taken this job a couple of weeks earlier. Josh had imagined working one on one with people, listening to their concerns and thoughtfully advising them on the best solutions to consider. He certainly had not imagined calling up random sales victims to promote the flavor of the month.

When Josh had accepted this position, the twenty-four-year-old had been excited about finally working in the promising world of investments and finance. As a student at the University of Wisconsin-Madison, he and his buddies had formed an investment club for fun, throwing their money into trading options through college. Josh discovered how quickly one could make money and how much more quickly one could lose it. But at the time, he didn't mind—this was just a side project. He was majoring in international relations and political science, with an emphasis on economics, and when he graduated, he began working in sales support for a multinational pharmaceutical company.

As a new graduate, Josh had a clear plan: make enough money to be financially secure and live a comfortable lifestyle. The son of a single mom, Josh grew up in a modest but comfortable home in the suburbs of Chicago. Still, he started working as a newspaper delivery boy for the *Chicago Tribune* when he was just eleven. Although he didn't *have* to work, he wanted to earn his own money to buy things an eleven-year-old craves: candy, cassette tapes, a boom box. As he grew up, he gravitated toward activities that allowed him to help and educate others. Even as a junior counselor at the local YMCA summer camp, his goal was to be the best at whatever jobs he was assigned. And his father always told him that if he could do that, some of the rewards might be financial.

It all seemed to be going according to plan. Josh thrived in the sales and marketing division of the pharmaceutical company, and within two years, he was on the fast track, running a program with an annual budget of twenty-eight million dollars. He loved the job, loved helping the sales reps and physicians get what they needed to succeed. But after a year and half, Josh began to see another side of corporate life, one in which office politics meant that his hard work didn't always get recognized or rewarded. He was disheartened, but when he was offered a promotion to be a pharmaceutical sales rep in Boston—prime territory for pharmaceutical sales—he jumped at it. This amazing opportunity would turn things around, Josh told himself. Moving to a new city where he didn't know anyone was a scary thought, but he had just ended a long-term relationship. Maybe this was a sign that it was time to chart a new course.

❯ ❯ ❯ "Is this really it?" Josh said aloud as he viewed apartment after apartment in Boston. Everything within his budget was old and shabby. With outdated appliances, no elevators, and just window air conditioners,

Josh felt as if he had taken a step back in the world. For the same amount of rent, he could still be living in the shiny new high-rise overlooking Lake Michigan that he had just left. Nothing here was at all like home, Josh thought with a pang. Although he had gotten a small pay increase with this move, it wouldn't cover the higher cost of rent, food, and gas, nor would it allow him to save the way he had planned, if at all.

Josh sat on the edge of the bed in his hotel room. He shrugged his shoulders to release the tension and allowed himself to think the words he had tried to ignore for weeks: *This move is a mistake.* It wasn't just the apartments or the city. It was the job itself. Not only that, he realized as he sat alone in that hotel, he didn't really want to be away from his family and friends and all that was familiar to him. He smiled as he thought of his family back home. His grandmother was still alive, and Josh appreciated their close relationship. Even though his parents had divorced when he was young, his parents and their new spouses ensured that Josh always felt supported and loved. His father was his chief mentor, and his stepmother was warm and kind—nothing like the stereotype. His mom—hardworking, intelligent, and beautiful—was a single-mom success story and Josh's biggest supporter. When she remarried, her husband didn't try to take Josh's father's place, but instead became a great friend and role model. Why, Josh wondered now, had leaving everyone he loved seemed like a good idea?

His stepfather, Frank, asked the same thing when Josh called home that evening. "So why did you express such excitement and interest in the job if you didn't want to move?"

It was a question Josh hadn't been willing to contemplate too deeply at the time.

"It was a good opportunity," Josh said. Even to him, the words sounded hollow.

"Maybe, but maybe not a good one for you," Frank said.

"Not a good opportunity for me," Josh repeated, exhaling as he let that phrase wash over him. A tiny bit of the tension he had felt for weeks lessened. He was known as a go-getter, and this job was a go-getter's dream. How could he turn it down? *Be honest*, he thought. It wasn't right for him. And even if it was a good career move, even if it seemed like a dream job, didn't he get to say no, if it wasn't the best direction for him?

"I guess I was flattered that the company would select me," Josh admitted. "And I was drawn to what I thought was the glamour of being a successful sales rep here in Boston." After a moment, he sighed. "I was wrong."

"Then come home," Frank said.

With an unfamiliar feeling of defeat, yet a sense that it was the best move for him, Josh made a call to his supervisor.

"You're what?" his supervisor asked incredulously. "Josh, do you know how many of our sales guys would kill for that territory, but you want to throw it away?"

Josh steeled himself for the disbelief, the censure. "It's not what I thought it would be," he tried to explain.

"Not what you thought? You've only been there a few days!" his boss replied. But Josh knew deep in his heart that going to Boston was the wrong decision. Time wouldn't change that. As hard as it was to break the news to his company, the fact that he felt calm and at peace with his decision reinforced that he had made the right one.

Naturally, his family and friends welcomed him back. Most praised his decision, though a few buddies razzed him about his sudden change of heart. "Not the right opportunity for me," Josh explained, repeating his stepfather's words. Still, he felt a little embarrassed that he had made the mistake of heading to Boston before knowing enough about the reality to gauge whether it was right for him or not. It didn't help that his company wasn't pleased with the change of events.

"Do you know how much paperwork we had to go through to get you that opportunity?" Josh's boss asked him when he returned to his old job.

Wow. I thought I was a little more valuable than paperwork, Josh thought. After all, if he were useful enough to send to a great territory, wouldn't it be worthwhile to make sure the fit was right? Still, determined to work hard and be the best, Josh jumped back into his old position with zest.

After he had been back for a few months and realized his company didn't appreciate him the way he initially thought they did, he started thinking about his next steps. He knew whatever move he made would include his new girlfriend, Tracy.

Tracy was a surprise. One of Josh's friends had given him Tracy's phone number soon after he returned to Chicago. Josh had never been set up and had never called a stranger but he dialed the number. The first time he and Tracy talked, they stayed on the phone for hours. Not wanting to ruin a perfect phone relationship, and with both still uncertain how they felt about their respective recent relationships, they moved slowly. It was six weeks before Josh and Tracy met in person.

Yes! Josh thought when he first saw her. She opened her screen door with a big smile, and when he looked at her long, straight dark hair blowing in the wind, he couldn't help but think: wild child. Tracy was beautiful, tanned, and athletic. She was spontaneous. She was fun. She made him put aside his to-do lists and just *be*. With most people, Josh tried to look as though he had everything under control, but with Tracy, he didn't have to pretend. Heck, she didn't care if things were out of control—she just cared about him. Immediately, they were inseparable.

It was easy, then, to share his dreams with her.

"I'd like to start something new—something in the financial industry," he confided to Tracy one evening over dinner. She looked at him, quietly assessing what he'd said. Josh was always planning the next thing, the next goal. Heck, Josh had just completed real estate classes and passed his real estate exam just in case his current job didn't work out. While Tracy didn't mind meandering along the path, confident that she would eventually get where she needed to be, she admired his vision and drive.

"Why don't you talk to my brother?" she suggested. Her older brother, Scott, was in the insurance business.

"I don't want to sell insurance," Josh said.

"Well, maybe he knows someone who does what you're looking for," she replied.

Sure enough, Scott connected Josh with a boutique brokerage firm in a western suburb of Chicago a few weeks later. Josh was delighted when he met with the partners of the firm and they offered him a job. He felt so lucky to break into the financial industry. It didn't matter that the job worked exclusively on commission, that the office was a one-hour commute from Josh's downtown apartment, or that he had no industry experience. What he *did* have was an opportunity.

Then, his new boss showed him the white phone book and told him to write a damn ticket. Sell a mutual fund to every client, whether it was needed or not.

"How am I supposed to do my job well if I don't know the first thing about these people and I'm not in a position to make the best possible recommendations?" Josh asked. But his boss merely glanced at him with a "don't cause trouble" look.

When Josh was growing up, his father always shared "life lessons" with him. Every situation was a learning opportunity, even the ones Josh would have preferred to be just dad-and-son time. But most of those lessons sunk in, and Josh thought about them as he contemplated the phone book.

The Golden Rule was a big one. Treat others the way you want to be treated. Would *he* want to be sold a mutual fund that wasn't the most appropriate, given his age, desired level of risk, income, or savings objectives? No! So why should he treat potential clients differently?

What about valuing people? Listening to them? Josh thought about the response he'd received from his boss when he returned from Boston. He didn't feel valued—not as an employee and not even as a person—when the major complaint was that Josh's return resulted in more paperwork.

"How's it going, Josh?" Scott asked, checking in on him one day.

Josh and Tracy had recently gotten married, and her family spent almost all of their time together. They worked in different businesses but the same office complex, so they ate lunch together every day. They also had a family dinner every Sunday. Scott was six years older than Josh, and they spent a lot of time together, enjoying each other's company.

"It sucks," Josh said bluntly. "I thought I was going to be in a training program. I'm barely making any money. I don't feel like I'm even helping anybody. Except my bosses."

"Well, I'm getting ready to introduce a new insurance program nationally that you might be interested in," Scott said.

"I don't want to sell insurance," Josh said.

"Before you decide, why don't you listen to the details?"

Josh paused for a second before nodding. "Go on."

"With this program, we'll send out mailers to potential clients about various topics, like how to avoid probate or maintain privacy or reduce taxes. If they turn the card in, we can make an appointment and go visit them. You'll be leading with the insurance, but you'll have the opportunity to talk with them about other types of investments, as well as estate planning," Scott said.

Despite his initial misgivings, Josh began to feel excited. That entrepreneurial spirit and confidence that had been beaten down since the failed Boston move began to revive.

Josh's brokerage firm adopted the insurance program Scott had designed and brought in some of the country's top insurance producers to train Josh and his peers in the office. Josh's boss announced to the entire sales team that Josh would likely be the first to fail in the program since he was new and too young to connect with retired people.

Although Josh didn't respond, he took notes. He would never intentionally denigrate anyone who worked with him. Relying on his inner strength and resurging confidence, Josh used his supervisor's words to fuel his fire and desire to succeed. He threw himself into his work, sometimes driving three hundred miles a day in all parts of northern and central Illinois, only to be stood up at a prospect's front door or to sit with people at their kitchen tables and listen to their life stories. However, his hard work began to pay off: it wasn't long before Josh was the top-producing rep in the office.

"I appreciate the opportunity to talk with you about your financial and family concerns," Josh said to Ron Jones, a seventy-year-old retired schoolteacher. Recently widowed, Ron was interested in avoiding probate for his family if he were to pass away. Evelyn, his wife of more than forty years, had been sick for eight years before dying of cancer. Ron knew the toll her illness had taken on him and his only daughter, and he wanted to make sure that when his time came, his daughter would have an easier time.

"I don't want the government to take more than its fair share of what Evelyn and I worked so long and hard to pinch together. Besides that, I want to make sure my insurance will cover everything I might need—nursing home, hospice, home care," Ron said as he placed a glass of water in front of Josh.

"I can absolutely help you with that," Josh assured him. "What other concerns do you have?"

Ron looked at Josh thoughtfully. "What do you mean?"

"Perhaps you have questions about what happens if the insurance doesn't cover all of your expenses," Josh explained. "Or how to make sure you have enough money to live comfortably. Or you might need to take a new look at how much you're paying in taxes or the risk you are taking in your investments. We can look at your entire financial picture, not just at one aspect of it, like insurance, to make sure you're in good shape with your money."

Ron nodded slowly. "That might be good."

What a different feeling that was, Josh thought, with pure satisfaction, as he backed out of Ron's driveway several hours later to head home—a hundred miles away.

Over the course of the next few weeks, Ron and Josh discussed what Ron really needed. They looked at what he had and built a solid plan that would suit him and his family. This was what Josh was supposed to be doing: helping people recognize the questions they had or should have—and then working with them to create solutions. For the first time in nearly two years, Josh felt his career was on track. It wasn't about the money, he thought. Well, not *all* about the money. It was also about doing what he was passionate about—educating people and helping them do what they needed to do with confidence.

Shortly thereafter, Josh decided to move his office from the western suburbs to the northern suburbs, near Scott and the rest of his family. Josh and Scott began working together more regularly and learned about a series of workshops they could teach to retirees called Lifelong Financial Security. Once the two of them completed an intense training program, they could conduct their own workshops on financial topics. No more driving hundreds of miles to visit with people! Instead, people could register and pay a nominal amount to attend a four-week course at the local community college, where they would be educated on risk and investing, taxes, long-term care, and estate planning. Josh found that his natural instinct to teach served him well, and that he enjoyed being in front of the class and easily connected with the students. While many of these attendees were very knowledgeable and thirty to forty years older than Josh and Scott, they still had many questions. The students needed reassurance that they understood things properly, and they needed someone to educate them. Josh began developing a more holistic approach to financial planning, asking tough questions: how could he give clients advice until he really knew them? How could he know what their needs were if he didn't understand all aspects of their lives? Suppose, for example, he'd only given Ron Jones the insurance he asked for, instead of delving deeper and considering the other areas with which Ron was concerned? As Josh became more steeped in the philosophy of the holistic approach, he knew this was the way he wanted to do business. He wanted to educate clients and help them understand what their money was or wasn't doing for them, in order to help them match their financial decisions to their larger life and family goals.

In 1997, Josh and Scott started a business together, which they named Retirement Planning Group. All of the lessons Josh had learned in his life helped form what he wanted in their new company. He and Scott would treat people as individuals and with respect. They would take the time to educate clients on their finances and help them devise a plan that would meet their specific goals. They would make recommendations based on what the individual client needed, not just on the investment flavor of the month. By understanding his clients' needs and putting them first, Josh was convinced they would be successful.

CHAPTER 2

THE BEST LAID PLANS

"SOMETIMES WHEN YOU LEAST EXPECT IT, THE TABLES TURN
AND THAT SCARY FEELING THAT HAS TAKEN HOLD OF YOU
FOR SO LONG SOMEHOW TURNS INTO HOPE."
David Archuleta, *American Idol* Finalist 2008

She'd had a plan. It was a good one: earn a degree in finance and marketing from DePaul University. Find a good job at a financial company. Help an organization reach its goals, and reach her personal goals at the same time, eventually owning her own business. Along the way, get married, and later, have 2.5 children and live the "white picket fence" life she'd fantasized about as a child. Check, check, check, on-the-way-to-check. Everything on her list was getting checked off, so why, Nicole wondered, was she so miserable?

No doubt, it stemmed from the conversation she'd had with her supervisor, Jim, that morning.

"Nicole. Come here," Jim had called in his typically abrupt fashion as she passed his office on the way to hers. She had come in early as usual, preferring to start the day before many of the other advisors had arrived, while the office was still quiet. Then, sitting at her desk, she could slowly sip her water while she reviewed her clients' files and prepared for upcoming meetings.

But her morning ritual would have to wait. Nicole stepped into Jim's office and sat down in the visitor's chair, laying her laptop case on the floor beside her. Jim sat behind his oak desk, fingers busily tapping his computer keyboard.

"What's up, Jim?" she asked, hiding her wariness.

"You saw a new client yesterday, a Mrs. Simons?" Jim glanced over at Nicole.

"Yes, it was my second meeting with her," Nicole said. "I took her through a financial plan, and she wanted some advice on her portfolio. She's a widow and wants to make sure she stays conservative in her investments," Nicole responded, smiling at the memory.

In her late sixties, Helen Simons had a quick mind, combined with a self-deprecating humor that had made the meeting delightful. As they talked, Mrs. Simons explained that before she retired, she taught public school for forty years. She would have taught in an old school style, Nicole immediately envisioned. Strict, but dedicated and caring. She would have made sure her class learned all of the multiplication tables, knew the states and capitals, practiced perfect handwriting skills, and knew the lessons they would need later in life. Nicole eased her elbows off the conference table and sat up a little straighter in her chair. For the rest of the meeting, Mrs. Simons had treated Nicole as warmly as she would a granddaughter. She'd shown inherent trust that Nicole would not steer her in the wrong direction.

"What did you recommend to her?" Jim asked Nicole.

Nicole leaned forward. "Well, she didn't need much alteration in her portfolio. She doesn't need to take on more risk at her age. She needs to ensure she has enough liquidity for an emergency, so I told her that we would recommend reducing some of the volatility in her portfolio by getting out of the single stock holdings that her husband held."

"What about the annuity?" Jim asked.

Nicole shook her head. "No, I don't think that's good for her. It's a seven-year back-end charge annuity, and she's already sixty-nine years old. I don't want her to have to tie up her money for that long. Also, if she requires the money, she'd need to have access to everything."

"So you didn't even suggest it?" Jim asked.

"Jim, I know that this annuity may be a great one for many of our clients," Nicole said. "But I don't think it's the right one for her."

"Nicole, you've been with us for three years, correct?" Jim asked.

Nicole nodded. "Yes, right out of college."

"So you understand how we operate. We all work on commission, and you are going to starve. You need to hit your numbers if you want to qualify for your benefits and keep your health insurance. Nicole," Jim warned, "you are never going to make it in this business."

When Nicole had first joined the firm, the idea of working at one hundred percent commission wasn't daunting to her. She had set high expectations for herself all of her life, so the demanding goals were a welcome challenge. But the way the company was structured, Nicole learned, was that her senior managers earned a percentage of any commission she made. Some products she sold, like annuities, earned more commission than others did, and Nicole could tell that those were the ones she was being steered to recommend.

"I understand where you're coming from, Jim, but as a financial advisor, I have to consider the best interest of my client," Nicole said. This was not the first time Jim had questioned her investment advice. It wasn't a concern that her recommendations were misguided; it was more that they wouldn't be as profitable for the company.

"Of course," Jim said. "But at least let your clients know what their options are."

"Of course," Nicole echoed as she left.

Walking to her office, Nicole looked calm on the outside, but she was fuming inside. How *dare* he imply that she was doing her clients a disservice by not pushing an investment that wasn't right for them? She entered her office, closed the door behind her, and sank into her seat.

This was not the plan. One of the aspects Nicole enjoyed most about helping clients with their finances was teaching them about their investments and helping them make a plan that might actually improve their lives. In college, she'd taken classes in investments and fell in love with the idea that she could help people put the pieces of a puzzle together to ensure their financial health. Starting this job, that's what she thought she'd be doing. But now, it was clear—her job was to sell whatever the company had, not necessarily what was best for clients. Her job wasn't to teach. Or to advise. To keep doing what she had been—helping people like Mrs. Simons maintain the savings they had worked a lifetime to earn—might earn her more carefully worded reprimands from her boss. It might even get her fired. Nicole knew from talking to co-workers that her company was no different than others in the industry. Changing companies wouldn't make a difference; if she chose not to accept the status quo, she would have to change careers entirely. The only one that excited her was the thought of teaching.

Nicole could imagine explaining her crisis of conscience to her family. They would be supportive of a career change, she knew, but they would be shocked. Nicole had always charged forward in life, sure of her next step. Maybe it was because she was the middle of three children, and both siblings had special needs. Her older sister had behavioral and mental disorders, and her younger brother had autism; growing up, both required a lot of her parents' attention. Although her home was loving and caring, it was also chaotic. Nicole could never predict what disruption of routine, sudden noise, or other irritation would spark a meltdown from one of her siblings. As a result, she tried to be self-sufficient so her parents could focus on her brother and sister. Even as a twelve-year-old, Nicole began her bid for independence, placing flyers in her neighbors' mailboxes, offering to babysit, pet sit, or do chores. Nothing was better than riding to the bank on her bike, jeans pockets stuffed with coins and bills to deposit into her account.

Although Nicole knew her parents would ultimately support any career decision she made, she wasn't sure how her husband, Ken, would react. He was returning to school himself, and their plan had been that she would support them while he resumed his studies. Once he was done, they would both work until they eventually had kids and figured out how to balance the two-job family life. But there was no way that Nicole could support them both and pay for his schooling on a teacher's salary.

"You need to give up that dream of having the perfect job," Ken said when she described her frustration. "Work isn't meant to be fun. That's why they call it work. But maybe it will be better at a different company. You don't make enough money now as it is. You're meeting with all these clients and not selling the products that make you money."

"From everything I've heard," Nicole argued, "I really don't think it *will* be better somewhere else."

"Well, we have a mortgage and car payments, Nikki. We have responsibilities to take care of, even when one of us is having a bad day."

A *"bad day"? Why can't it be possible to be fulfilled in your job?* Nicole wondered. *I don't want work to control me. I want to have a family* and have fun with my friends. But I don't want to sell my soul to do it. I want to have it all: the fulfilling career, great marriage, and happy and healthy children.

"I feel like a used car salesman," Nicole said to her parents one Saturday, as Nicole and Ken sat around the kitchen table on one of Nicole's rare free weekend mornings. "I can't put my integrity aside just to make a commission. I've had interviews for a few positions in marketing and human resources, though not in investments. I've started filling out applications for master's degrees in teaching programs. I'll go part time." Nicole shook her head. "I think I have to give up my dream of being in the financial planning business. I'm clearly not cut out for it."

"You've talked about being unhappy for months now," Nicole's mother said, pausing to stir her oatmeal. "I think you're right to look at other options, and you've always liked teaching. At the end of the day, Nikki, everything always works itself out. Look into everything, go on interviews, and apply for a master's program. Educate yourself on all your options."

"Nikki, do you really think we can afford for you to go to school now?" Ken asked. "You already have student loans, and I'm going back to school. You have a degree, and I think you need to figure out how to use it and make sure we can pay our bills, the way we agreed. I'll do my best to help out while I'm in school, but let's face it: my program is full time, and what I make won't pay the mortgage." He looked at her pleadingly. "You have so many connections. Why not use them to find work at another company? What's the big deal?"

Nicole looked down at her now-cold oatmeal. No matter how many times she tried to explain things to Ken, he just didn't understand. Nicole felt more lost than ever. The person who was supposed to support and encourage her was the one who made her feel completely alone. *I just wish I had a clear vision of my future to know what will make me feel happy and fulfilled*, she thought once again.

With Nicole's silence, Ken pushed his chair away from the table and wandered into the family room.

"Nikki don't get discouraged. There may still be a solution," Nicole's father said, pouring another cup of coffee. "You should call Scott. In fact, I just saw him last week and told him that you weren't sure if you were going to stay in the business or not. He could give you some advice."

Scott Loochtan owned an insurance agency and had been friends with Nicole's parents for years.

"You said you didn't think the situation would be different at any other firm," Nicole's father said, as if reading her mind. "But maybe Scott can give you some insight into whether that's true. I know he's in insurance, but I believe he has a business partner who does financial planning. Maybe he can connect you with him."

"Dad, I don't know. It just seems like every company out there is hawking products to any breathing person. You know that's not for me." Despite the early hour, Nicole suddenly felt very tired. "I just don't want more of the same, Dad," she said, unsure of whether she was just talking about her job.

"Nikki," her father said gently, "just give him a call and see what advice he can give."

Nicole pondered her father's words for a moment. She ducked her head, slowly sipping her water so her parents wouldn't see the rare tears in her eyes. The conflict was pulling her like a stretching machine. This was not how her life was supposed to go.

"Okay," she said. "I'll call him."

When Nicole called Scott, he suggested that she meet with his brother-in-law, Josh Kadish. "Josh and I started our business, Retirement Planning Group, about fourteen years ago," Scott explained. "I handle the insurance part, and Josh covers the investment side. I think he'd be the right person to talk to about what you'd like to do. Josh does things differently than others in this business," Scott said, somewhat cryptically. "I'll tell him to expect your call."

It most likely wouldn't lead to anything, but Nicole decided it wouldn't hurt to give Josh a call. That afternoon, as she looked at Scott and Josh's company website, she noticed their emphasis on the educational process of planning and a focus on building relationships with their clients. Nicole called the office number, and when she gave her name, she was immediately put through to Josh.

"Nicole, Scott told me to expect your call," Josh greeted her.

"Yes, I'm interested in picking your brain a little bit about the industry. Scott says you operate differently than other firms," Nicole said. Her voice was calm, not betraying her wariness. She didn't want to be sold—she just wanted to know the truth about this business. Could she do what she enjoyed? Was it possible to make decisions for her clients that were in their best interests, or would she always have to be selling something?

"We do. Why don't we talk about this at lunch one day next week?" Josh suggested.

A few minutes later, Nicole hung up the phone, with a calendar event penciled for eight days later. She would find if Retirement Planning Group was, in fact, different from competitors, different from her company.

Even as she planned for her meeting, she reminded herself that it might not work out. From her online research, she knew that Josh was young and successful. She found articles about him in *The Wall Street Journal* and *Crain's Chicago Business*. But just because he was well known didn't mean they would share the same philosophy. She would go in there with her eyes wide open. She would ask tough questions and listen carefully to his answers. She wouldn't get too hopeful. She was not going to set herself up for disappointment this time.

CHAPTER 3

SERENDIPITY

"VITAL LIVES ARE ABOUT ACTION. YOU CAN'T FEEL WARMTH
UNLESS YOU CREATE IT, CAN'T FEEL DELIGHT UNTIL YOU PLAY,
CAN'T KNOW SERENDIPITY UNLESS YOU RISK."
Joan Erickson, Author, *Islands of the South Pacific*

Josh sat at a quiet corner table at Claim Jumper Restaurant in a northern suburb of Chicago. Almost a decade and a half after entering the financial services industry, Josh had built a thriving business with almost more clients than he could handle. People gravitated to his educational and holistic approach to financial planning, and although the company had expanded to include other planners and support staff, no one worked with clients quite like Josh. If he'd had less energy and passion, he would have burned out long ago.

"You've made yourself indispensable," Tracy pointed out one evening at home. That may have been too true. Josh wished he could slow down. He knew he could use less stress and more family time—something Tracy reminded him of on occasion. He and Tracy had two boys, eight and ten, and they treasured family time. Going to the boys' basketball games was the highlight of Josh's week. The couple also loved taking the boys away from the gray skies and cold weather of Chicago to sunny, warm places like Arizona, Mexico, or Grand Cayman, where they could all relax and enjoy simply being together. But it was hard for Josh to completely unwind. Being "indispensable" had its drawbacks, and when Josh wasn't at work, he worried that clients might need him, so he kept his phone nearby and charged; even on vacation, he checked his email constantly and called in to the office sometimes five times a day.

When Scott had suggested that Josh meet a family friend to see if she might be a good fit for the company, Josh was intrigued. From the beginning, Josh had a clear vision of the way he wanted to run the business, but recently, he wanted something more. He never felt comfortable telling people what he did because it was hard to explain. When people heard that he was a financial planner or wealth manager, they assumed he was like most—focusing on investments and the performance of the stock market. It was frustrating to be boxed into that same category; Josh knew investments were just a piece of what he and his team did. They also tailored and delivered financial plans to their clients. They listened to what people wanted to accomplish and educated them as to how to get there, financially. Josh and his team didn't just talk about investments but were also well versed in tax, estate planning, and insurance. They worked hard to be a one-stop resource or "concierge" for all of their clients' life needs, and they were rewarded for their stellar service and deep-rooted relationships they formed with their clients. Most clients were referred to Josh from their current or former employer, an outplacement firm, a CPA, or an attorney. Usually expecting the typical financial advisor-investor relationship, clients were pleasantly surprised by the breadth of services and experience delivered by the Allworth Financial team. Josh always said that the company wanted to provide Four Seasons service with FedEx efficiency.

The ultra-wealthy have something called a "family office," where a private company manages investments and trusts for a single family whose net worth might exceed $100 million. Josh hoped to make that same type of comprehensive and holistic service available to the families who worked hard and lived comfortably, yet still worried about their financial future. Nevertheless, he was missing something—a leap or a surge that would propel his business to the next level: helping clients connect with their own life visions in a meaningful way.

Josh had built a sizable practice based on trusting relationships with individuals, CPAs, attorneys, outplacement firms, and Fortune 500 companies that understood the importance of addressing the financial part of life. He could both thank and blame David Blaydes for that. David's relationship was the one diamond-in-the-rough that emerged from Josh's early brokerage experience. David had mentored and worked with Josh nearly ten years earlier. After working in the financial services business for fifteen years, David had a wealth of knowledge and contacts. He kept his business growing by routinely conducting seminars and workshops for Fortune 500 employees who were being outplaced. He tapped Josh to join him, which was the catalyst that led Josh to conduct seminars for employees of corporations, outplacement candidates, and the public.

But David did something much more important than teach Josh how to conduct seminars. He taught Josh the importance of balancing family and work.

Early in their relationship, Josh watched David and his four kids mark his calendar with an "X" on the days they were off from school, when David was going to take off work and spend the time with his family.

Years later, when Josh and Tracy had their first son, David made sure to remind Josh that it was most important to carve out family time, rather than keep working ten- or twelve-hour days six days a week.

David also fed Josh's desire for continuous self-improvement and business growth. The two of them made the decision to work with a life and business coach to help guide them to real success and happiness . . . *True Wealth!*

Josh looked up to David. He was hugely successful, highly respected, and had a way of communicating the normally dry and boring topics of finance and estate planning in a manner that was entertaining and captivating. David, in turn, appreciated the passion, hunger, and determination that Josh exuded. His drive and confidence was rare, especially in a person in his mid-twenties. David would smile when he looked at his young apprentice, seeing an image of his younger self.

As Josh and David worked together to conduct educational workshops for Fortune 500 companies, they spoke about their hopes to do more together in the years ahead. David was successful but never satisfied. He was convinced that he would one day grow his business exponentially. He just needed the framework to do it. Enter Peak Productions, a life and business coaching firm headed by one of the top financial planners in the country. This kind of coaching would be just the edge David thought he needed. Explaining to Josh what this service offered, David said, "It's part psychologist, part business strategist. You have to envision your future and set goals."

Josh nodded. But he was thinking, *I do that already.*

"What is your value proposition to your clients? What do you offer that's different?" David continued.

"I see clients as individuals," Josh said. "I'm not just trying to sell people something. I want to help them really understand their goals and then create a solution that will help them be happy. Not just financially." It wasn't just about financial management or security, after all. It was much more encompassing, much more emotional, than that. It was about helping people evolve as humans and then guiding them to find a way of supporting that evolution with their finances. Josh always knew that his approach to financial planning was different than others in his industry, but he had not thought about the vastness of the opportunity that he had to help people tangibly improve their lives.

In 2005, Josh and David began participating in the Peak Productions coaching program. Ron Carson was an industry legend and managed close to five billion dollars. His coaching program helped planners improve their skills while providing a guide to building a very efficient wealth management practice. Despite building Allworth Financial to a level of great success with consistent annual growth, Josh wanted more. More business. More structure. More goals. A roadmap to achiev-ing true happiness by working every day to ignite the inner passion Ron Carson says everyone has. As Josh completed the "Blueprinting program's exercises"—goal setting, future vision, rewards, and more—he felt a growing excitement for the future. Life was getting better and better, and Josh was able to see and appreciate it as it was happening. He was excited to share his experience with his team and others around him.

Some team members were reluctant to dig into the deeper life questions. "I help our clients with their investments. What does my personal life have to do with anything?" some asked.

"We're doing great here, Josh," others said. "We don't need to change anything. Let's just keep doing what we're doing."

Fine. Josh couldn't change everyone in one day or by himself. But he truly believed that the team was in a position to control its environment and build a great culture in which everyone would truly enjoy coming to work and strengthening relationships with all the folks they served. Josh would eventually make change, one nudge at a time. He was a man on a mission. Although it wasn't ideal, he knew that pioneers often spent many years out in the world, alone.

❂ ❂ ❂ Nicole walked briskly over to the table the hostess had pointed to and smiled at the brown-haired man looking up at her.

"Josh?" she asked.

"Nicole!" Josh stood up and shook her hand warmly. "Very nice to meet you."

Nicole sat down across from Josh. "Very nice to meet you, too," she smiled as they exchanged small talk about the unseasonably warm weather.

"Scott told me a lot of good things about you," Nicole began. "He said that you have a different approach to investments and planning."

"We do. And Scott told me that you're working with an insurance company doing financial planning, but that you're considering something different?"

Nicole studied Josh for a moment. With a light pink oxford shirt and dress pants, he looked both confident and approachable. What did she have to lose by being honest?

"I've been working at an insurance company for three years, since I graduated, and I've been disappointed because the emphasis has been so much on selling insurance products even though we can supposedly advise on everything," Nicole explained.

"What's wrong with that?" Josh asked, a smile in his brown eyes.

Uh oh. Maybe Scott was wrong about Josh. Maybe this firm was just like all the other ones.

"That's not helping the client!" Nicole said, exasperated. "People need to be educated on their finances. So many clients I've worked with don't understand where the money they have is coming from or going to, so they can't make the best decisions. When I thoroughly help a client develop a plan, my managers get upset with me for spending too much time with them. But that's what I'm supposed to do."

"So you enjoy teaching people." Josh said. "Why?"

"Because it empowers them," Nicole replied. "You know that saying:

give a man a fish and he'll eat for a day. Teach him how to fish and he'll eat for a lifetime? Well, I want to teach my clients to fish, not just give them one. I want to help them be in their best financial position and not just make a commission that pads my bank account. I want to do for others as I would do for my family and myself. I don't want to lie awake at night worrying because I put my clients in a product that I would never buy and would never sell to my family."

Josh leaned back in his seat. This was interesting. For the first time in fourteen years, he was talking with someone who spoke the same language as he did—someone who shared the same passion, drive, and vision. Although he initially intended this meeting to be just a favor for Scott, he was surprised by the conversation. Maybe this could lead to more?

"Why don't we order?" he suggested. "And talk some more."

Throughout lunch, Josh and Nicole asked each other questions, probing to understand each other's insights and motivations. Why had Josh started the company with Scott? How was Retirement Planning Group different from its competitors? What were Nicole's personal values?

"I really like planning for people," Nicole summarized as they finished their meal. "I'd love to be able to go out and find the best of what is available and make sure that clients have it, and that they receive impeccable service. Again, for me, it's about treating others the way I want to be treated."

"The Golden Rule! I live by that and it's refreshing to hear you feel the same," Josh said, describing his epiphany about helping clients focus on life purpose rather than on pure financial success. "I am committed to helping our clients plan for their financial future. And as for making specific types of recommendations, our firm is fully independent, which means we aren't influenced to push a particular company or product. That's one of the significant differences between us and other firms in the industry. We *can* go out and find the best of what is available for individual clients."

Nicole couldn't help smiling. "Your company sounds like a great place." To be honest, Nicole was envious. To work in a place where passion and purpose were combined—that was what she wanted. Although this was just an informational lunch, Josh was asking some fairly probing questions. Nicole didn't allow herself to think that his deep inquiry might mean something more for her.

Although Allworth Financial *was* pretty great, Josh thought as they finished dessert, it wasn't yet where he ultimately envisioned it could be. But maybe with the addition of someone who shared his ideas and energy, that could change.

"It was a pleasure to meet you, Nicole. Let's stay in touch," Josh said as they walked to the restaurant door.

As soon as Nicole got to her car, she called Ken. "It went really well! I still want to try to be a planner. There's a whole side of this business I didn't know about," she gushed when he answered.

"All you've been talking about is how all companies in the financial services industry are the same," Ken said. "You want to change jobs? Go ahead. You've got offers on the table for big corporations with big benefits. You need to stop searching for ways to do financial planning. Just accept one of the big company job offers so we can stay on track."

Nicole hung up the phone, shaking her head. They came from two different worlds. For Ken, a job was just a means to a paycheck. It wasn't an identity or a measurement of progress. He couldn't understand her perspective, and she couldn't conceive of not having her job be an integral part of who she was. Despite Ken's pressure to take one of the job offers, Nicole held off on making a decision, hoping that Josh would be in touch.

Several days later, Nicole's phone rang. It was Josh, and he explained that there was a job opening available for an advisor.

After a few more conversations and a formal interview, Josh offered Nicole an opportunity to join the team at Allworth Financial Despite her excitement, Nicole was nervous. *The grass isn't always greener on the other side*, she reminded herself. This job presented an enormous amount of risk. Was it going to get her any closer to her goal of owning her own practice and running her own business so she could do things the right way? The doubt that she encountered at home didn't help either. "Why would you take that job? There's no guarantee of even a paycheck!" Ken argued when she told him about the opportunity. On one hand, Nicole understood his fear. She was giving up one offer of $80,000, and until she had established herself at Allworth Financial, she wouldn't make even half of that. She still had college loans and other payments due. But on the other hand, this was a chance to attain her dream. She had hoped it was possible, but she could actually see it happening now. Ken wasn't happy, but Nicole knew she had to do this. *I'll give myself one more shot to live my dream, to do what I'm passionate about*, she thought. *Five years. That's how long I have to make it a success. And if it hasn't happened then, I'll find a job in traditional corporate finance.*

"I accept," she told Josh, with butterfly wings batting in her stomach. She thought even if it only lasted one year, if she could say she exhausted every effort to live out her passion, if she could learn a few things from Josh that she could carry forward—then she would consider it a success.

❯ ❯ ❯ In her first weeks at Retirement Planning Group, Nicole realized what Josh already knew: the two of them shared a similar view of the world and of wealth management. Because of that, Josh took Nicole under his wing, grooming her for increasing responsibility. As a new advisor, it was sometimes awkward when she was invited into client meetings with Josh when more seasoned advisors were not.

"I don't want to make waves," Nicole began.

"If I wanted them in here, they'd be in here," Josh said. He understood that some employees' feelings might be bruised, but for years, he had hoped to find someone who shared his vision, and now that he had, he wasn't going to let office politics get in the way of developing the company.

As much as Josh welcomed Nicole to share the work, he also realized that having her there meant he had to give up some of it. In those first months, she shadowed him, and as they met with clients, she explained that she and Josh would be working together and that clients could contact either of them. Still, Josh would sometimes look startled to see her enter a client meeting, as if he had forgotten that he was no longer alone.

"Josh, we have a receptionist, right?" Nicole asked, stopping by his office one day as he hung up the phone.

"Yes. You know we do. Why?"

"Because I've seen you have so many interruptions during your day," Nicole said. "I know you want to be responsive to clients—we both do—but sometimes those calls are simply scheduling appointments. Those interruptions take you away from your real work with clients."

"Go on," Josh said.

"Well, can't our receptionist handle those kinds of calls?" Nicole continued. "And can't some of our advisors handle some questions clients have? I mean, we want to be responsive, but we can do that as a *team*, not just as Team Josh," she said with a chuckle.

Josh's immediate reaction was no, he needed to talk with the clients himself. But that wasn't really true for about thirty percent of the calls he received. Shifting those calls could give him time to do more critical work, while still ensuring all of his clients were getting responses. Josh felt a slight lifting of the burden of being indispensable.

"You're right," Josh said. "Let's give that a try."

Nicole realized that her instincts were right: Retirement Planning Group was different from her previous firm. She had a voice, and the people around her now were happy to listen to it.

"It's like going to a shoe store and saying I need a size nine in these black pumps," Nicole explained to Ken. He was still not happy about her job decision, and she kept trying to give him examples of why this was a good move. "And the store says, 'I'm sorry, we only have brown and they come in size seven, but you are going to stick your foot in it, and it is going to fit you, even if it doesn't.'" Nicole shook her head to banish the memory of her previous experience. "Now I can say, 'Oh, you want black pumps? Great! What fabric? Would you like ones with a pointy toe? Rounded toe? What size do you need?' Now we can customize it completely."

But Ken wasn't convinced. "Nikki, I get that you're passionate about this, but at the end of the day, this is going to turn up just like your old job." Now Ken shook his head. The idea of a company that encouraged people to live out their dreams was foreign to him, and he was worried that Nicole would be crushed with disappointment. But she was no longer worried.

Nicole brought enthusiasm, keen perception, and a strong desire to get things done, Josh thought as he waited for her to come into his office for their morning meeting. He didn't intimidate her. On the contrary, she was comfortable laughing with him or even poking gentle fun at him when she thought he was taking himself too seriously. It was surprising when she came into his office with her head down and eyes suspiciously wet.

"Nicole? What's wrong?" Josh asked with concern.

"I'm so sorry, Josh. I didn't mean for this to happen." She took a deep, unsteady breath and then blurted, "I'm pregnant. I know I've only been here four months, and I swear I didn't know I was pregnant and it wasn't intentional. I mean, we wanted to have kids someday, but not now! I still have my own school loans, not to mention Ken's. This is just not the best time to have a baby. And Ken is still contentious with me about taking this position, so we were in no position to get pregnant anyway."

"Here, sit down." Josh came around his desk, and they sat side by side in the two chairs before it. Unlike many men, Josh wasn't uncomfortable with female tears. He handed Nicole a tissue and waited until she was comfortable speaking again.

"Look, Josh." Nicole wiped her eyes and sat up straight. "I understand if you don't think this will work out."

"Nicole, I brought you on board because I saw the potential in you," Josh said. "Nothing has changed. You are one of the hardest working people I've ever met, and I have confidence that you'll be with this firm for a long time. This isn't a bad thing. It's a bump in the road that you didn't expect, but we'll work it out.

"And, by the way," Josh added with a smile as Nicole rose from the chair, "Congratulations."

⊙ ⊙ ⊙ As if to prove to herself and everyone else that her pregnancy wouldn't diminish her productivity, Nicole threw herself into her job, learning intently, making suggestions, and helping implement new ideas. Not only did she want to ensure that her role at Allworth Financial would be fulfilling and financially rewarding, but she also wanted to prove to Ken that this had been the right choice all along. She spent an hour of her labor on a phone call with a client, and three days after her son Gavin was born, Nicole was in the office for a short meeting.

"Why are you here?" Josh asked in surprise when she came in.

"It's just for a few minutes," she said.

Josh shook his head. She was becoming indispensable, too.

That past December, six months after Nicole had started, Josh and his family had gone on their traditional winter vacation. But this time, instead of checking into the office every couple of hours, he only called once a day, increasingly confident that the company could survive without him—for a little while, at least. It was progress.

⊙ ⊙ ⊙ "So, Josh, what do you do?" asked the tall man standing next to Josh at the networking event.

"I'm a partner at Retirement Planning Group," he answered.

"Oh! You help people who are getting ready to retire. Well, nice meeting you." The forty-something-year-old professional swiftly walked away toward another potential contact.

Josh shook his head. That wasn't the right answer to the man's question. But Retirement Planning Group was the name of the company. It just didn't reflect what the company did. Not anymore.

"I think we need to reconsider our image," Josh announced to Scott and Nicole, about a year after Nicole came on board. "We're giving people the wrong impression about what we do. They think we just work with people who are retiring, so we're potentially missing a huge audience of potential clients. If someone isn't thinking about retirement, they don't think they need us."

"I agree," Nicole said.

"I like the name. It has history," Scott said.

"Maybe there's a way to blend the history with where we're headed," Josh suggested.

Josh, Scott, and Nicole began working with a local consulting company called Wisdom Link, which was referred by another Peak member. The Wisdom Link referred to itself as an intellectual property development company and had similar values to Peak: living out your passion, identifying your wisdom, telling your unique story, and making a positive impact on those around you—goals that Josh, Scott, and Nicole embraced. As the trio began describing their company, their vision, and their purpose, they gained insights that helped define what they wanted their company to be.

"Allworth Financial," Josh proclaimed proudly as he unveiled the new logo in a PowerPoint presentation to the team. "We help people who are in transition. It *could* be someone who is retiring, but it doesn't have to be. It might be someone between jobs, getting divorced, or whose spouse has died."

"It could be an adult child with aging parents," Nicole added. "Or someone with a sudden influx of wealth. Or it might even be people who have come to a point in their lives where they need a second opinion to make sure they are on the right course to reach their goals."

"Change is difficult, and we help people through the process. But even more importantly, we help people connect their wealth to their life's purpose," Josh said. "*That's* our mission." He looked around the room and felt the energy surge as the staff began to take in the details of the next slide, the new website.

"We're not so much changing what we've been doing; rather, we are packaging it and explaining it more clearly," Nicole said.

One of the new client tools described on Allworth Financial website, LifePrinting, was adapted from the life coaching information. Why not pass this golden nugget on to clients since it had such a positive impact on each of them personally and shaped the growth opportuni-ties that the team was experiencing? In order to help clients connect their wealth to their life's purpose, clients would have to figure out what that purpose was. Another new tool they would use was the LifePrint Navigator—a system to help clients and their families have all essential information and contacts at their fingertips in case of an emergency.

Allworth Financial. Josh looked at the logo on the screen. Educating clients. Navigating them through transitions so they could make future decisions with confidence. Maybe even guiding them to discover a greater purpose and then helping them achieve it. Yes. His personal values, his work values, and his vision coupled with the vision of the team . . . everything was coming together, at last.

CHAPTER 4

THE VALUE OF A SECOND OPINION
CLIENT STORY: BOB AND DEBBIE NORTH

"NOTHING DIMINISHES ANXIETY FASTER THAN ACTION."
Walter Anderson, Author, *The Confidence Course*

Bob North shifted in the uncomfortable waiting room chair. Actually, he thought, it wasn't the chair itself that was uncomfortable—it was waiting to see his doctor.

Bob had never liked any part of a doctor's visit, from the time the appointment was set, to leaving his office in the middle of the day for the examination, to the invasiveness of the exam itself—even if it was just to draw blood. Fortunately, Bob had enjoyed good health, although at his last visit two or three years ago, his doctor mentioned the extra ten pounds he'd gained since his visit two years before *that* and warned him about pre-diabetes. Once he reported that back to his wife, Debbie, she had been after him to eat more vegetables, cut back on his favorite pasta dinner, and nagged him to exercise more (forget about his occasional cigar). "The least you could do is get out of the golf cart and walk!" she'd say, exasperated, with her hands on her hips. Even after forty years in the United States, her words still held the faint rhythm of her native England.

"Yes, dear," Bob would reply sarcastically with a grin. After thirty-seven years of marriage, he recognized her nagging as caring, and she recognized his sarcasm as reluctant acquiescence.

But then his father, Dean, suffered a fatal heart attack, and Bob began rethinking his own health and future. As he shuffled through magazines on the table next to his chair, he shook his head. He still couldn't believe his dad was gone. At eighty-five, Dean always seemed much younger. He had become a father at a young age and always treated Bob more as a brother than as a son. Active and seemingly healthy, Dean had been playing in a doubles match at the club when, right after winning the match, he felt clammy and dizzy and collapsed. He never woke up and was pronounced dead at the hospital.

"He died doing what he loved," Dean's second wife said at the funeral, partly to comfort Bob and partly to comfort herself.

On an intellectual level, he knew his stepmother was right, but he still sometimes felt adrift without his father as an anchor. *How bizarre*, he thought as he flipped through a magazine—*to be an orphan at the age of sixty-two. Move on*, he ordered himself briskly. Debbie had warned him he'd have those moments, those punches of grief that came out of nowhere. "There's no time limit on feeling better," she reminded him. Still, Bob would prefer not to have a breakdown in the doctor's office. He glanced at the receptionist, but since she had been brusque when he asked her five minutes earlier how much longer until he could see the doctor, he decided to try a new tactic that Debbie often recommended: patience.

Bob picked up a magazine and thumbed through it. An article caught his eye: "What are you retiring TO?" That was an interesting take, he thought as he started reading the piece. He had always thought of retirement as the time he was going *from* working, versus considering what he was going *to* during retirement. As a successful lawyer in a mid-sized law firm, Bob had finally reached the age where the mandatory buyout from his partners would take place over the next three years. Although he had a vague idea of what he would do after, truth be told, retirement was hard to envision. Sure, he could play more golf, but what else? Was more time on the green all he had to look forward to? The thought brought an unexpected wave of depression. Who'd have guessed that his impending retirement could trigger a late-life crisis?

The article mentioned a company called Allworth Financial, which described itself as a company of Life Transition Specialists who helped people figure out how to plan their financial futures. *Interesting*, Bob thought. One of the points in the article was to understand your investments and determine if they were in line with your goals. Bob and

Debbie had been diligent about saving. Once they had finished paying for their daughter's pharmacy school, Bob and Debbie decided to put the money they had been spending on tuition into investments and savings. Although Debbie ran the household budget, when it came to major expenses, Bob liked to be involved; he was the one who usually contacted their accountant, financial planner, insurance agent, or tax attorney. But he hadn't talked in-depth with any of them in quite awhile.

"Bob North?" The nurse stood at the doorway leading to the examination rooms. "Would you come with me, please?"

"Just one moment," he said, quickly reaching in his jacket pocket for a pen and a scrap of paper. *Allworth Financial*, he scribbled, then stuffed the paper back into his pocket. Maybe it was time for him to schedule another checkup. This time, the financial kind.

◎ ◎ ◎ A few days later, Bob called Allworth Financial. As a lawyer, Bob was familiar with doing due diligence before making most decisions, so he looked up Allworth Financial, Josh Kadish, and Nicole Mayer to gauge their experience. They had solid backgrounds in financial planning, and the company they ran together offered more services than many financial planners did, with CPAs, insurance agents, and estate planning attorneys available.

"Hi, Bob, how can I help you?" Nicole asked when she picked up the transferred call.

"I'm interested in a second opinion about my finances," Bob said.

"Well, if you'd like to learn about what you have and how to get where you want to be, you've come to the right place! We're passionate about helping people truly understand their finances and helping create a plan that allows them to live out their dreams," Nicole explained.

"I don't know about all of that," Bob said with a skeptical chuckle. "I just want to know if my finances will support me when I'm ready to retire, and if not, what changes I should make now. Also, I'm already working with an advisor that I am happy with."

"That's great," Nicole said, smiling. Bob, like many people who came to Allworth Financial for help, had someone they worked with and thought the issue boiled down to money. Most of them soon learned that the issue was about much more than dollars and cents. It was about dreams and purpose. But that recognition would come in time.

Nicole spent a few minutes getting some basic information from Bob. After hearing about his family situation, primary concerns, and general financial picture, Nicole had a better understanding of the challenge that would lie before her and her team. She took a few more minutes to explain the process that they would go through in their face-to-face meeting.

"My wife, Debbie, will be joining us," he added.

"Excellent. We recommend that couples do this together, especially when you're considering a major transition such as retirement. It gives both of you a chance to learn more about your financial situation, as well as how you envision this new world of retirement," Nicole said. "Also, remember that this process is meant to be educational, with no obligation to work with us beyond the initial meeting."

"That sounds great! So what's the next step?" Bob asked with excitement that took him by surprise.

"Well, I'm happy to shoot you an email with some background information on our firm as well as a couple of forms for you to complete so that we can prepare an analysis to review with you and Debbie. I'll also include you in the email distribution we send to our clients each week so you can get a feel for how we communicate and make ourselves available to our clients."

As Bob hung up the phone, he thought once again about his future. Debbie had been talking to him about retiring for the past couple of years. But when their investments had taken a hit in the economic downturn that went from 2007–2009, he was a little wary of making another move that could drastically change their finances too soon. Debbie, on the other hand, was more than ready for him to retire. She had retired from her job as a nursing administrator the previous year and was looking forward to the next stage of life with him.

"We said we'd do all the traveling we've been putting off," Debbie reminded him. "But you're still working fifty hours a week. If you don't do something soon, you'll be too exhausted to enjoy yourself when you finally do retire."

Bob considered his wife's words as they entered the Allworth Financial offices. Despite his initial enthusiasm after the phone call with

Nicole, he felt as if he were metaphorically dragging his feet as he opened the glass door to the receptionist area. He was always so sure of what direction to take in a legal case, but he felt stuck as he tried to figure out his own future.

After their phone call, Nicole had emailed him a couple of forms to complete, along with a workbook entitled *LifePrinting Exercises*. It was a series of questions designed to help him figure out what his passions were. Bob had gone through the questions, and while he would certainly enjoy more leisure time, he still wanted more than anything to be a lawyer. He had been one for more than thirty-five years. It was his identity. If he wasn't a lawyer, then what was he? Bob looked over at Debbie, who was giving the receptionist her name and making small talk. It was easier for her. She had an ability to adapt to circumstances with ease. When she retired, she had immediately filled her time by volunteering at the library and back at the hospital. She even took up Zumba. Maybe she was just wired differently. She had come to the United States in her early twenties, all alone, and stayed with family friends until she finished her nursing degree. Maybe she was just better prepared to deal with change, to be more adventurous, than he was.

"Bob—they're ready for us," Debbie said as she nudged his arm.

They were escorted to a bright conference room, made warm by the welcoming assortment of trail mix and chocolates, specialty teas, coffees, water, and bottled sodas. But nothing was better than the sight and smell of the freshly baked cookies that lay so perfectly on a platter in the center of the conference room table.

Moments later, a tall blonde woman walked in, followed by a dark haired man.

"Hi, Bob and Debbie. I'm Nicole." The woman held out her hand and shook each of theirs.

"I'm Josh Kadish," the man said with a friendly smile. After shaking hands and ensuring that the Norths had selected their drinks and preferred snack, everyone sat down at the conference room table.

"Bob, when we talked last week, you said you were interested in a second opinion as you contemplated retirement. What specifically is it that you are looking for?" Nicole began. Although she and Bob had discussed this over the phone, it was often useful to go through it again in person to make sure the couple was starting from the same place. The interaction also allowed Josh and Nicole to pick up on small details—facial expressions, body language, and interaction between spouses that might provide more information.

"Well, as I said then, I'm looking at retirement in the next few years, and I want to make sure I'm—we're—prepared," Bob explained. "I've accepted a three-year buyout and want to take a look now to make sure we have what we need for the future."

Nicole noticed Debbie tapping a finger rapidly on the table. Some dissension here, perhaps.

"Debbie, Bob said you've been retired for about a year," Nicole said.

"Yes. Originally, we were going to retire together, but with the economy, it made more sense to wait. I did, and now I'm retired, and Bob had planned to join me, but he seems to be putting it off, first with one thing and then the other."

"You make it sound like I'm delaying on purpose!" Bob said a little irritably. "I have good reasons to wait. Do you want to find out in five years that we don't have enough money? There's nothing wrong with being cautious."

"No," Debbie agreed. "But there's something wrong with not being able to move forward."

"You know what? That is exactly why you're both here," Josh interceded smoothly. "Once you know where you stand, you'll be in a better position to know how much flexibility you have in your timing for retirement."

"I brought in the information you suggested," Bob said, motioning to a folder. "I had more people to contact than I originally realized. I'd forgotten a savings account we had set up years ago when we lived in another state, and one of Debbie's old 401(k) accounts from a job she had early in her career, but I think it's all here now."

"This is perfect," Nicole said as she looked at the papers in the folder. "You used the worksheet I emailed you. I hope that simplified things."

"Yes. It was very comprehensive, actually," Bob said.

Some clients kept meticulous financial records and were able to easily transfer the information to a single, simple form that Allworth Financial provided. Some clients came in with a box of files and unopened envelopes of statements. In either case, Nicole and Josh assisted them in sifting through the information, making sure they thoroughly understood what each piece was for and what it meant.

"Bob, when we talked about our second opinion services, I mentioned that we want to understand what it is that you want to accomplish and educate you on what you have," Nicole said. "From there, we will point out where you are on track and where you may be able to make improvements. Our recommendations are tailored to you. At the end of that process, you are under no obligation to continue working with us. If you have financial relationships in place that you are comfortable with, we encourage you to keep them if they can help you going forward. Or you may decide to do nothing at all. That's up to you."

"You mean if you give us advice, we can go somewhere else to implement it?" Debbie asked.

"Absolutely," Josh said. "Just as you may have a physical at the doctor, think of this as a full financial physical. At the end of the examination, we'll understand your situation and give you a prescription that you can fill at the pharmacy of your choice."

Bob liked the idea of not being obligated to follow up with Allworth Financial. He might want to, but it was clear that Nicole and Josh were getting paid a one-time fee for their experience and advice. They weren't going to try to automatically convince him to buy some investment to generate a commission.

He looked at Debbie. He knew she was frustrated with him. For years, they had talked about their life after retirement. Then came the Great Recession, and he realized how easily his financial picture could change. He felt a renewed need for security—both financial and emotional. When his dad died, some of his friends urged him to retire right away—spend whatever time he might have left doing what he enjoyed most. But Dean's death made Bob feel insecure all over again. Now was certainly not the time to make major changes.

But it wouldn't hurt to know where he stood financially. Maybe that assurance would help him feel confident enough to take a tiny step forward.

"Where do we start?" he asked.

The first step was to develop a complete picture of the Norths' financial situation. Where were the investments, savings, insurance plans, real estate, other assets, and debts? Nicole and Josh used the spreadsheet Bob had filled out to explain each point.

"Bob, what are your plans after the buyout?" Josh asked. "What will you be retiring to?"

Again, the retiring *to*, not retiring from. Maybe there was something to be said for that viewpoint. "I don't know," he answered honestly. "It feels like everyone is rushing me out the door. Go ahead and retire already! But I still feel I have something left to offer. I don't want to just spend my days golfing. I still want to work!"

Debbie looked at him in surprise. "You still want to work? But why? That's not what we talked about. That's not what you said."

"I know, but I like feeling productive. I don't want to wake up in the morning and have to manufacture some place to go just so I can get out of bed," Bob explained.

"But you can just lie in bed and decide if you even *want* to get up or not! Doesn't that sound nice?" Debbie asked.

"Maybe for a few days, but no. That would drive me crazy," he admitted.

It wasn't unusual for couples to have different ideas or expectations about retirement. Even if they had similar views at one point, new feelings would sometimes begin to surface as they approached decision time. Nicole and Josh knew that although this may seem like a disagreement, it was an opportunity for Bob and Debbie to openly address the issue that was obviously bothering both of them.

"Bob—it sounds as if you see this as an either/or proposition. Either you retire and have nothing to do or you continue to work, with no time to spend as you'd like," Josh observed. "Are there any other options?"

"Such as?" Bob asked.

"Maybe you turn your attention to something that might provide you with fulfillment but might not take up *all* of your time. Maybe work twenty hours a week?" Josh suggested.

"Yeah! I bet you could find any number of organizations that would value your ability to provide legal advice, maybe on a volunteer basis," Nicole added.

"You could mentor," Debbie said. "Many colleges have mock trial programs and need someone to help them learn court procedures and how to form legal arguments. Or you could write a book or take on speaking engagements," she added, gathering steam.

Bob held up a hand. "Okay, okay, I get it. Maybe I have been thinking too narrowly."

"Maybe?" Debbie questioned, but patted his arm encouragingly.

"Bob and Debbie, have you thought about the lifestyle you'd like to maintain during retirement? Once we know that, we can help you determine how much money you'll need to have, and that will give you more insight to help you make decisions about your future," Josh said.

"What I'd really like is to have a maintenance-free life," Debbie said. "We live in the big house where we raised our family, but I could see us being in a condo in a few years. I'd like us to be able to walk out, lock the door behind us, and jet off somewhere fun just because we want to. We're young and healthy. I don't want to look up one day and find we're suddenly seventy-five, maybe not in good health, and saying 'I wish.'"

Debbie was almost breathless after her burst of speech. She knew her vision of leisure didn't match Bob's vision of continued productivity, but maybe if he considered somehow reducing his hours, they might have some room for collaboration.

Using Bob and Debbie's current spending as a guide, Nicole and Josh estimated how much the couple might spend during their retirement, taking into consideration future inflation, potential healthcare expenses, and milestones like college for their grandchildren and living to age ninety.

"This is simply a starting point and not anything set in stone," Josh explained. The analysis also took into account the assumed returns the Norths' investments might earn.

After reviewing the details of their overall portfolio, Josh raised his eyebrows.

"It looks like you could be taking on much more risk than you need to," he said, pointing to some particular investments.

Bob looked at the sheet. "Our financial planner suggested these investments and told me they were a good buy because I'd get a higher return."

"Higher return also implies higher risk," Josh explained. "The question isn't necessarily whether something is a *good* investment. The question becomes, is it an *appropriate* investment? Do you need to assume this higher risk? Can you afford to take this higher risk? Can you afford to lose money?"

Josh paused before continuing. "When the markets were down from 2007 to 2009, you lost a big chunk of your portfolio, and that heavily affected your retirement plans. On the investment side, our job is to become our clients' risk managers. Once we identify the rate of return you need, we manage your risk to attempt to achieve the rate of return with as little downside as possible. Don't get me wrong, our clients may have lost some during the recession, but we made sure that the risk in their portfolios was in line with their objectives and tolerance for risk."

"Not all of our recommendations are going to be about spending less or socking away more money," Nicole explained. "They may be about protecting against loss, saving on taxes, and maximizing your Social Security benefits. All of that helps keep more money in your pocket to get you where you want to go."

Bob sat back in his chair for a moment. Things were becoming clearer. It almost felt as though his father was standing over him, guiding him. A sudden sense of security enveloped him. He was on track to proactively chart his own course. He was ready to figure out what he'd like to retire *to*.

"So, what's the next step?" he asked.

SECOND OPINION: ADVICE FROM JOSH AND NICOLE

Many times, prospective clients come to us wanting only a checkup—they aren't looking for us to advise them on changing their financial strategy but are seeking reassurance that they're going in the right direction. When we offer a second opinion, they know that we are not trying to sell them any products since they have already paid for the review. Often, however, as we offer a thorough explanation and education on a client's financial picture, they start to consider coming to us for strategic direction. Asking, "What's the next step?" is a pivotal point, indicating that clients are ready to take charge of their financial future.

When we helped Bob and Debbie take a fresh look at their finances, we started with an expense worksheet. This allowed them to break down where and how their money was spent and invested. That microscopic view helped us determine specifics on investments and look for ways to help them save money in smarter ways, without necessarily having to spend less. The expense worksheet below gives you a start at looking at your own financial picture.

The next step was helping them more fully develop their vision for retirement. Many couples don't fully share with each other how they would like to spend their future, and therefore, they cannot plan for it. Once the vision develops, clients can see more opportunities for fulfilling it. Bob thought he had to keep working a full-time job, but once he realized that he had the finances to sustain him, he was more open to other types of job opportunities that would let him continue to be productive.

Social Security optimization was the third aspect we looked at with Bob and Debbie. Sometimes clients gain more money results by making adjustments in areas such as Social Security. By looking at the hundreds of potential claiming strategies and their implications, we can help clients select the combinations that have the potential to give them more money without having to buy an investment product, save more, or spend less.

For Bob and Debbie, working with an independent, holistic planner helped them integrate their financial portfolio and life goals.

HOW TO IDENTIFY QUALITY INDEPENDENT, HOLISTIC PLANNERS

1. They are held to a fiduciary standard.
2. They offer an educational process, not a sales process.
3. They charge a fee for advice but do not require you to implement their recommendations through them.
4. They are transparent regarding their fees and how they make money.
5. They are comprehensive in their knowledge of investments, tax, insurance and estate planning.
6. They provide 100% of their clients with a full financial plan or retirement analysis.
7. They ask questions in order to understand your needs and objectives.
8. They are educated as to what you have and where you are today.
9. They personalize a plan to tell you how much you will likely spend throughout your lifetime or retirement and provided guidance on

how to get there.

10. They tell you the probability of achieving your goals doing what you are today as well as other scenarios.
11. They formalize your goals and put them in writing for you.
12. They help you prioritize your financial opportunities.
13. They suggest suitable alternatives you may not have considered.
14. They provide you with a tax-efficient liquidation order of your investments in the event you need money.
15. They prepare a Social Security optimization analysis that details how and when you should claim your benefits to maximize your payout.
16. They review your tax returns with an eye to possible savings in the future.
17. They suggest alternatives to lower your taxes during retirement.
18. They reposition assets to take full advantage of tax law provisions.
19. They work with your tax and legal advisors to help reduce your tax liability.
20. They assist in preparing an estate plan for you.
21. They review all of your life, health, long-term care, disability, property, and casualty insurance.
22. They do not represent only one single company.
23. They follow their own advice and recommendations.
24. They provide you with a list of references.
25. They have proper credentials and designations (i.e., AIF®, CFP®, CDFA™, CFA, JD, CPA, etc.).
26. They have a good track record and clean disciplinary history.
27. They do due diligence on money managers and mutual fund managers in order to make appropriate recommendations.
28. They stay up to date on changes in the investment, tax, and estate planning world.
29. They monitor your investments.
30. They understand your personal life goals, not just financial goals.
31. They review your investments in your company 401(k), 403(b), or 457 plans.
32. They monitor changes in your life and family situation.
33. They proactively keep in touch with you.
34. They remain only a telephone call away to answer financial questions

for you.

35. They serve as a human glossary of financial terms such as beta, P/E ratio, and Sharpe ratio.
36. They review your existing IRAs.
37. They review and revise portfolios as conditions change.
38. They recommend investments outside of their own management.
39. They help you understand the risk levels in various investments.
40. They look "inside" your mutual funds to compare how many of their holdings duplicate each other.
41. They record and researches your cost basis on securities.
42. They speak directly to your attorney, CPA, and insurance agent to ensure everyone is on the same page and provide a system for checks and balances.
43. They determine the risk level of your existing portfolio.
44. They help you consolidate and simplify your investments.
45. They allow you to track ALL of your holdings in a single place including those they do not manage.
46. They provide you with suitable alternative investment options.
47. They show you how to access your statements and other information online.
48. They shop for CD rates from financial institutions throughout the country.
49. They offer investments that are FDIC insured and guaranteed.
50. They review your children's custodial accounts and 529 plans.
51. They suggest alternatives to potentially increase your income during retirement.
52. They make sure their firm delivers excellent service at all times.
53. They provide referrals to other professionals such as accountants and attorneys.
54. They listen and provide feedback in a way that a magazine or newsletter does not.
55. They use their years of experience to offer some of the top strategies.
56. They help educate your children and grandchildren about planning, investments, and financial concepts.
57. They help with the continuity of your family's financial plan through generations.

58. They facilitate the transfer of investments from individual names to trust, or from an owner through to beneficiaries.
59. They keep you on track.
60. They identify your savings shortfalls.
61. They develop and monitor a strategy for debt reduction.
62. They educate you on retirement issues.
63. They educate you on estate planning issues.
64. They educate you on college savings and financial aid options.
65. They are people you can trust and get advice from in all your financial matters.
66. They are an experienced sounding board for ideas you are considering.
67. They help implement recommendations.
68. They are honest with you.
69. They connect your financial means to your larger life meaning.
70. They help you accomplish your long-term goals and dreams with confidence.

CHAPTER 5

THE BOMB WAS DROPPED
CLIENT STORY: TOM AND LYDIA JENSON

"THE SECRET OF LIFE, THOUGH, IS TO FALL SEVEN TIMES AND
TO GET UP EIGHT TIMES."
Paulo Coelho, Author, *The Alchemist*

"We're going to have to let you go."

The words were abrupt, but even as they echoed in Tom Jenson's head, he knew his boss's brevity was meant to be kind. *Don't draw it out*, HR had probably advised. At least, that's what HR had told Tom when he'd led a downsizing in his own department a few years back.

"The department is being restructured, and to avoid redundancies, several positions are being eliminated," Allison said from behind her desk, her back to her picture window view of Lake Michigan. With keen insight and an easygoing sense of humor, Allison had made her way through a male-dominated industry. But she wasn't laughing now. She looked pained.

Tom sat back in his seat and exhaled, feeling as deflated as an old tire. He had worked for Midwest Chemical Company for twenty-seven years and had seen his share of employees come and go. He just never thought he would be the one ushered out the door. In this moment, he couldn't think of a thing to say except, gesturing to the window, "Looks like a beautiful day out there."

Blinking, Allison turned her chair around and followed Tom's gaze. For a second, they both stared at the reflection of clouds on the water. Then, gently, Allison handed Tom a folder full of information about managing the next phase of his life, including insurance coverage, career counseling, and financial planning.

"Midwest would like to offer you outplacement services to help you plan your next steps. It's a generous package, and HR will discuss it with you during your exit interview," she said.

And that was that. Tom accepted the folder and numbly left Allison's office. After a lifetime dedicated to the company, after countless geographic moves that he had reassured his family would be well worth it, this was how it would end.

Looking down so he would not make eye contact with anyone, Tom walked down what seemed to be an endless hallway until he finally reached his office. Just inside the door, he noted the commendations on his credenza, given to him over the years by the company that had just fired him. He had to get out of there. He grabbed his computer bag and shoved his laptop inside—could he do that? After all, it was the company's, not his. Damn it! He was taking it home tonight anyway. No one had said he needed to clean out his office today. Reflexively, he stuck the folder Allison had given him inside a compartment of his bag. *Think step by step, Tom*, he thought. *Just get through the next step.* He checked his pockets for his cell phone. Yes. Keys? Yes. With one last look at the project files on his desk, he turned to leave. He wanted to go home before anyone said anything to him, before anyone looked at him, before he broke down. Then maybe he could start making sense of what had just happened.

In the parking deck, Tom sat with his car idling. He thought about calling his wife, Lydia, but he couldn't, not just yet. His thoughts swirled, but he kept picturing the face of his son, TJ, a decade ago, when TJ was nine and Tom had explained that the family needed to move from Georgia to Oklahoma because of work.

"But, Dad, what about my baseball team? I don't want to leave my friends!" TJ had just started pitching on his house league team, and he lived for the weekly games with his best buds.

"I'm sorry, pal," Tom told him. "One day, it will be all worth it." TJ had eventually nodded, his face downcast as he resigned himself to an uncertain future. Now, Tom imagined that his own face looked like TJ's did ten years ago, trying to not to cry even as life gave him a wallop he hadn't seen coming.

❍ ❍ ❍ Later that week, Tom pulled his car into the parking garage of what would become his new "office" in a nondescript office park in the Chicago suburb of Oakbrook. As he turned off the engine, checking once more to make sure he had a pen and paper in his folder, he glanced up and saw Phil Brody, another vice president, walking through the door of the outplacement firm. *Phil, too?*

After his meeting with Allison, Tom had refused to call any of his co-workers to find out who had or had not made the cut. Either he'd feel jealous of those who hadn't suffered the same fate as he did, or he would feel a sense of justification that someone else was miserable, too. Either way, it wasn't a good testament to his character. But Phil? He had been one of the top salespeople in his division before becoming sales manager and then VP. Even though rumblings and rumors about Midwest's financial stability had begun a year earlier, Tom still thought people like Phil and him were safe. Tom shook his head. It wasn't his job to worry about the company's employment decisions anymore.

Tom walked into the outplacement office and up to the receptionist, an attractive older woman with silver hair.

"May I help you?" she asked, smiling.

Tom leaned in so his voice wouldn't carry. "My name is Tom Jenson. I'm here for the outplacement workshop."

"That's great," she said warmly. "The session will be starting in just a few minutes. You can go on in." She gestured to a large room on the left. "There's coffee and donuts, so make yourself comfortable."

The conference room held about thirty seats. Phil looked up as Tom entered the room, and they exchanged a nod before Tom walked toward the table that held several large coffee urns and cups. Tom added sugar to his coffee. *If only life were as easy as just adding sugar to make it sweet*, he thought. As men and women began to file in, Tom stirred his drink and made his way next to Phil.

"You too, huh?" Phil saluted Tom with his own cup of coffee.

"After all these years," Tom replied.

Phil nodded. "Chewed up and spat out."

"Good morning." A man in a crisp navy blue pinstripe suit stepped forward and addressed the group. "My name is Adam Lewis, and I will be your coach during your transitional period." He smiled, his teeth gleaming in contrast to his nut-brown skin.

"Many of you are here because of circumstances beyond your control. You've suffered a loss, and we are here to help. Your company has hired us to guide you through this transition so it is as short and positive an experience as possible."

As Adam described the types of assistance available, Tom waited impatiently to learn about the career counseling. That was what he needed the most. At fifty years old, he knew that starting over at another company would be difficult, and he had important financial obligations. With TJ in law school and Laura in college, Tom wanted to make sure that he could continue to pay their tuition, including sending Laura to graduate school in two years as promised. His salary at Midwest had been well into the six figures, but he knew that most companies would prefer to promote from within or hire someone younger from outside who would work for less. If a company did hire someone at his salary, surely it would be someone younger, someone who would be with the company for a longer time. These were obstacles Tom needed to overcome to continue providing for his family—to be the hero they expected and deserved.

Tom jotted down notes on a yellow pad as the career counselor came forward and spoke about the services provided. Tom's kids kept trying to get him to write notes on an app on his phone or iPad, but he was still a pen and paper guy—one more sign that he was becoming a relic. The counselor mentioned resume writing. Tom wrote that down. It had been years since he had needed a resume. Working in the same company for so long, performance reviews and personal recommendations were more important in moving up the corporate ladder. Tom wrote down ideas to highlight on his resume as the next presenters began.

"When you lose your job or are laid off, what do people say to you?"

Tom glanced up. A new man stood at the front of the room. He took the time to look around the room, making eye contact with people in the audience. With short brown hair, in a tailored dark suit, the man's warm smile and open gaze made him both professional and approachable. Like an older version of TJ, Tom thought.

"People don't know what to say," said one man sitting on the aisle.

"They avoid saying anything," offered another man from the other side of the room.

"They tell you that it's an 'opportunity,'" one woman said, making air quotes for the word opportunity.

"You don't see it as an opportunity?" the man in the suit asked.

"Well, no!" the air quoter said. She looked around the room to gauge support. "This isn't something I chose. I didn't ask for my company to get bought out by our competition. I didn't ask to get trampled as if I were worthless." She stopped abruptly. "Sorry. Still raw."

"Of course. That's human." The man nodded as he addressed the group. "And most people don't relish the idea of their life changing without their permission—of things happening that are beyond their control. But there is also something about these situations that can be liberating, forcing us to reevaluate what we want out of life. That can actually open up avenues, ideas, and yes, opportunities." He playfully did an air quote as he shot the woman a quick smile and glance. The air quoter gave a reluctant half smile.

"My name is Josh Kadish," the man continued, "and I am a Life Transition Specialist. Our firm has been engaged to be your one-stop educational resource during your transition and beyond."

Josh knew that these workshops were often a lifeline to employees who were still going through the stages of grief over their job loss, even for those who had expected it. He looked forward to conducting these workshops, even though the candidates were sometimes initially angry and defensive. But he knew the information he provided could help clients make such positive changes; the transformations were truly uplifting.

"You will likely have questions about your cash flow and budgeting," Josh explained to the group, "as well as what to do with your 401(k) and pension plans, and how to handle your lost life insurance, disability, and health benefits."

Tom's pen froze above his legal pad. He hadn't realized there were so many other aspects to think about. He had just been concentrating on how to land the next paycheck as soon as possible.

"Life Transition—what?" asked Phil.

"Life Transition Specialist," Josh repeated. "My job, my passion, is to educate you and help you navigate through this change or other life changes so that you can make future decisions with confidence."

"Sounds a little like hooey to me. Transition specialists? I don't get it," the man sitting in the aisle said. "No offense."

Josh nodded with a smile. "None taken." Outplacement candidates were often skeptical about his title, at least until he explained it in a way that resonated with them. He took a moment to look at each member of the audience.

"At different points in your life, you're in a transition," he said. "Graduating from college, getting married, having children, or retiring . . . these are all changes. They present a time to reassess the status quo. They are a movement from before to after. The transition can be difficult. It can be bumpy and full of surprises and disappointments. Or it can be smooth, filled with new paths of discovery. Most often, it's a combination of both, but our job is to help you take charge of the transition instead of it taking charge of you."

"I looked your company up on my phone here," Phil spoke up importantly. "You guys do financial planning. What does that have to do with 'life transition?'"

"I'll answer that, but let me ask you a question first." Josh paused while Phil nodded. "You asked what financial planning has to do with life transition. Some people whose lives change through something like a corporate downsizing want their lives to continue just as they were. They want to find a similar job, with a similar income, and pick up where they left off, in a sense. But others, when they have time to be introspective, begin to realize that they may want to live their lives differently. Do they really want to take another high-level job, with lots of travel and stress that takes them away from their family? Or do they want to start their own consulting business? Do they want to retire?"

Tom was rapt. He had assumed he would seek a similar replacement job and continue on as he had before. He had not considered any alternative.

Josh continued speaking. "Once people begin answering those questions about their transition, the next issue to determine is whether their financial situation supports what they want to do. I do want to make it clear to all of you in this room: we are not here to build a sales-oriented relationship with you. Instead, we are here to be an educational resource to you. We are paid to educate you and tell you what's in your best interest. While we can do all that financial planners or advisors can do, make no mistake—they can't do all of the things that we can do. Our entire organization specializes in working with people going through a life transition . . . just like you."

"I just need to plan how long I can be without a job without dipping into our retirement savings," Tom said, somewhat surprising himself. "I'm not looking for any major changes. I just want to get through this without going broke."

"I understand that," Josh said, nodding. "And that's an important concern that we are happy to address with you. But many people who are in a transition, who are at a decision point, find that this is a unique chance to recalibrate and set new goals. They realize they have many productive years ahead, and now that circumstances have changed, maybe some of their plans should change, too.

"Having the rug pulled out on your career is horrible, no question," Josh continued. "But maybe now is the time to ask yourself some life-defining questions."

"Like what?" Tom asked, almost defiantly.

"Like how much money do you need to be truly happy? Do you know what you currently have and whether it is sufficient for where you are today? Is it enough for where you want to be tomorrow? What if something happens and you become incapacitated or, even worse, pass away? Do you have things in order? What about taxes and planning for Social Security or COBRA or signing off on that separation agreement from your company? Are all of these issues being addressed so that you are working to support your true goals? And do you know what those are?" Josh paused as the attendees looked at him thoughtfully. "If this is something you'd like to explore, if you have questions or want to meet individually, complete the form in front of you and we'll connect. If you are interested in digging a bit deeper inside yourself, we're passing out a workbook that you can complete on your own time." Josh reached back at the table and began passing out thick workbooks entitled *LifePrinting Exercises*.

"Feel free to share these exercises with your spouse or significant other," Josh suggested. "Remember, they're going through this, too."

Guiltily, Tom thought of Lydia. He hadn't wanted to burden her with his worries, so he'd been quick to change the subject anytime she tried to open a conversation about losing his job. Now he wondered if that avoidance was just causing her more stress.

"Inside these workbooks," Josh continued, walking around the room, "you'll find questions about your core values—what's most important to you and your family—and how you envision your future, as well as some goal-setting exercises.

"Finally, we want to help you get through this transition as smoothly as possible, and networking is a huge part of that. Feel free to connect with us on LinkedIn and view our contacts. If there is someone in our network that we know who may be of help to you, we are happy to make the introduction," Josh finished.

At the end of the meeting, Tom was surprised by how thought provoking and reassuring the session had been. It was nothing like he expected from a financial planner. He expected to be sold products and hear talk about rolling over 401(k) plans, but there was none of that.

Tom stared at Josh's business card as he walked back out to the parking garage. Already, the sense of possibility that had started to bloom was dissipating. Josh's ideas were interesting, yes. But Tom didn't have the luxury of rethinking his future. He just had to get it back on track.

◐ ◐ ◐ "Live your life differently," Tom scoffed at the kitchen table later that day.

"Excuse me?" Lydia looked up from the piece of chicken breast she was cutting.

"Today, at the meeting, this guy said that now is an opportunity to live life differently. As if now is the time to go back on everything I've worked for," Tom said as he stabbed his fork into a piece of roasted potato.

"That's ridiculous. Surely you can't go in a completely new direction," Lydia agreed. She reached over and patted Tom's arm. "But with your experience, I know you'll find another job soon."

Lydia was always the optimist, Tom thought, while he was the pragmatist.

"When we're not paying a hundred thousand dollars a year in tuition for the kids, we can think about living life differently," Tom said, continuing to think aloud.

"What do you mean? Do you want to live your life differently?" Lydia asked a little sharply, briefly imagining Tom foregoing his corporate career to join a rock band. Silly, she knew, but although she tried to seem calm and sure for Tom, she was beginning to worry about their finances, too. She hadn't worked in years, and if Tom couldn't find a job soon, she didn't know what they'd do. Tom had assured her they had some savings to tide them over for a while, but how long was that, exactly?

"Well?" Lydia repeated.

"Huh?" Tom blinked, looking at his wife.

"What would you do differently if you could?" Lydia prodded.

Tom sighed. He just wanted to finish dinner and watch a little ESPN, followed by several of his favorite forensic crime shows, but he recognized that look in Lydia's eyes: she wanted to have a conversation.

When they were in college, he and Lydia used to go to the park near the university, spread a picnic blanket on the grass, and talk for hours about their dreams. Lydia had always wanted to teach. She said she had little dreams: a classroom of her own, where she could help five- and six-year-old children discover the magic of reading. Maybe one day, one of her students, all grown up, would find her and tell her what a difference she had made in his life. Tom dreamed of taking care of his family, but he spent more time imagining himself as an important executive in a company, where people would respect him for his keen insight. Well, he was doing the first part. And he had done the latter, for a long time at least. For all it was worth.

"If I didn't have tuition to pay, I would sell this house and move to a condo in the city for the summer and get a place in Florida for the winter," Tom blurted, surprising himself. But it was true. He hated Chicago winters. "What about you, Lydia?" he asked. "I don't know what you want to do."

"That's because it's been a long time since you've asked," she said, raising her brows. "In twenty-seven years, my answer hasn't changed: move back to North Carolina. Maybe to Wilmington, to live in a little house near the beach. With a screened-in back porch!" she added.

"I didn't know you still wanted to do that," Tom said. "You haven't said anything . . ."

"And when would I?" Lydia asked with a laugh that didn't sound entirely happy. "You were so involved in your career, and even when I taught, you made a lot more money than I did, so it made sense that my career took a back seat to yours. Then, once the kids came along, I had even less of a voice. It just seemed easier to go with the flow. I couldn't ask you to give up your career because I wanted to live in another part of the country."

Tom sighed and took a sip of his beer. "It's all screwed up, isn't it?"

Lydia reached across the table to pat his arm again. "Not at all. You're a good man, Tom, and you've done a good job for your family. We made a plan twenty years ago, and it's worked for us so far. Now may not be the time to change it, even if there are other things we want."

"You may be right. But maybe it wouldn't be a bad idea to talk to those Allworth Financial people to see what our options are. Just to know," Tom said. He searched Lydia's face. Although her hairline was now sprinkled with silver, her heart-shaped face and pool-blue eyes looked the same as when he first fell in love with her. "What do you think?"

Lydia shrugged. "Well, if you think it might help, I imagine it couldn't hurt."

Tom nodded. "I'll call tomorrow and schedule an appointment. And," he added, "I think you should come." She didn't know anything about their finances, and surely the conversation would go completely over her head. Tom read the reluctance in her expression and shook his head.

"That's okay. I'll go on my own," he said.

Is it time to do things differently? Lydia wondered. *Not just him, but her, too?*

"No, let me know when it is. I'll be there," she said, "and we can plan together."

Tom smiled. "All right. Let me show you some of the material they gave us at the meeting." Tom stood up from the table and walked to his office with a spring in his step that had been missing all week.

◎ ◎ ◎ Inside the office at Allworth Financial, Josh and Nicole took a final look through the Jensons' financial analysis. After Tom called to schedule a follow-up appointment, Nicole and Josh sent the Jensons a few forms to complete before their meeting—forms that helped detail the Jensons' savings, investments, retirement, life insurance, property, and debt, as well as how they viewed risk and their long-term goals.

"They did a good job of getting their information together quickly," Nicole remarked. "They're really motivated to learn more about their financial situation." Nicole felt a surge of anticipation. Clients who worked hard to pull together information were usually eager and open to learning.

"When I first saw him in the outplacement meeting last month, he was still shell-shocked about losing his job," Josh said, remembering how feverishly Tom took notes. Josh recognized that need to do something in order to keep the fear at bay. "I talked with him yesterday to confirm this meeting, and he sounded much more purposeful, in charge."

"Well, he'd be used to having projects and challenges. This process may have helped him regain his balance," Nicole suggested. "Nothing like a little financial hunting and gathering to bring back the honor!"

With a soft knock on Josh's door, Beth Grandin, Allworth Financial's Client Experience Concierge, poked her head in. "I've got the Jen-sons here. They're in the small conference room."

Tom and Lydia were surprised to see a fifty-inch plasma screen welcoming them by name, and they appreciated the warmth Beth exuded as she offered them a selection of snacks and drinks. Josh and Nicole entered the conference room and saw Tom and Lydia sitting next to each other at the oval table. They were both smiling but slightly nervous, Josh noted immediately, seeing Lydia's tightly clasped hands on the conference table. The mood in the room was tense, but not angry, much like the natural uncertainty of going to the doctor to get a checkup but not the results of a test.

"Hello again." Josh stepped forward to shake Tom's hand and greeted Lydia with a handshake and a smile. Nicole introduced herself and everyone exchanged greetings. After everyone sat down, Josh began the meeting.

"Since this is the first time we're meeting you, Lydia, I think it's important for us to take a step back and properly introduce ourselves and our services to you," Josh said.

"We would also like to hear about how you are handling this transition and the concerns that you have," Nicole added. She and Josh knew that this provided couples a time to air their frustrations, fears, and concerns—often ones they had not even shared with each other. She watched the couple closely to pick up nonverbal clues. Lydia smiled at

Tom while he introduced himself to Nicole—a good sign of a positive relationship. Tom brushed his hand on Lydia's arm, another sign of the warmth between them. Some couples weren't always so friendly, but Tom and Lydia showed a long-standing affection that would go a long way.

Josh and Nicole were like two peas in a pod, Lydia noticed, almost finishing each other's sentences. That easy camaraderie made Lydia feel a little more at ease, and she settled back in her seat, unclasping her hands.

"We're not doing so bad," Tom began.

"It's been very difficult," Lydia said at the same time.

The couple looked at each other.

"Do you really think it's been bad?" Tom asked in surprise. "I told you I would take care of everything."

Lydia sighed. "I know. But I worry about you. You take on so much, and it's keeping you up nights. You don't want me to worry, so I try not to let you know how I feel."

Tom sighed. "I guess we haven't done a very good job of communicating," he said, directing his reply to Josh and Nicole.

"What is it that's keeping you up at night, Tom?" Nicole asked.

Tom shrugged. "I keep running through different numbers, looking at our finances and wondering if we have enough. And wondering what I'll do if we don't."

"That's the number one worry of most people, Tom," Josh said. "One of the things we believe is essential is to ensure you understand your financial picture. We're not here to sell you anything. We're here so that you can be knowledgeable about how your money supports or doesn't support your goals."

"That's really the building block," Nicole added. Nicole met Lydia's doubtful look with an understanding one.

"I've never really paid much attention to our finances," Lydia admitted. "Tom takes care of that."

"That's okay, that's why you're here," Nicole said, and spent a few minutes explaining how they would review the financial analysis.

"Tom," Josh said, "when you called to arrange an appointment, you said that you and Lydia had recently talked about what you might like to do now that you're no longer with Midwest. Can you tell me more about that?"

Tom cleared his throat. "We talked a little about what we'd like to do if we had the control. Like, if we didn't have to pay our kids' tuition. For some reason, that opened up some ideas for me. I've felt constrained by this obligation. Don't get me wrong," he added, "I promised my kids I would do this for them, and it's important to me. But somehow, thinking about my life beyond it made me consider other alternatives."

"Other alternatives like what?" Nicole probed, leaning forward. Her ears always pricked up when clients hinted at unlived dreams.

"Moving somewhere warm," Lydia said.

"Having time to enjoy ourselves," Tom said, blushing slightly. "I've been thinking about the time I've spent at Midwest and although I have a great family, I can't help but think that I wasted too much time on that company. I'm fifty and healthy right now, but am I supposed to drive myself into the ground with work until I'm not healthy? When do I get to enjoy my life?" Tom took a breath, somewhat surprised by his own outpouring of emotion.

"What do you see as keeping you from doing that?" Josh asked.

"Money," Tom said bluntly. "Before Midwest let me go, I had planned to retire in ten years, but now, I don't know if I can. I sure don't want to be grinding it out at sixty-five or seventy. And yet, I want to enjoy my retirement without pinching pennies. I've worked since I was twenty-two years old. I think I deserve it."

"We think you do too, Tom," Nicole said. "What we want to do is help you figure out how to use what you've got to get what you want."

"Let's look at the financial information you gave us," Josh suggested. He reviewed each form with them thoroughly, asking and answering questions as needed. At one point, Tom got up to refill his coffee, and Josh directed a question at Lydia.

"Oh, you should ask Tom," Lydia answered. "He's the one who makes the decisions on our investments."

"But wouldn't you like to understand what those decisions mean?" Josh asked.

"I know times have changed, but when Tom and I were first married, we were very traditional," Lydia replied. "He handled the money, and I handled the house and eventually the family. Investments, portfolios . . . it's all so complicated. I think I may be too old to learn."

"That's bull," Tom said, looking at Lydia sternly as he returned to the table. "You're the smartest woman I know. Why couldn't you learn? It might be kind of nice to make decisions *with* you, instead of just telling you what I think we should do."

"I don't know." Lydia shrugged and looked at Nicole for support. "It's just overwhelming."

"You're right," Nicole said, her agreement surprising the couple. "It can be, but it doesn't have to be. Josh and I believe in helping our clients understand all aspects of their finances. We believe in educating you so you can make the best decisions, even if that means teaching you how to spell I-R-A." She smiled as everyone laughed. Even as Lydia chuckled, she recognized the sincerity in Nicole's eyes and realized Nicole was holding her accountable.

"Let's look at this information and see what financial picture it forms," Josh said. "Lydia, and you, too, Tom, we want to make sure you understand every aspect, so please ask lots of questions."

As Josh and Nicole reviewed the Jensons' profile, the couple began to ask questions.

"How long can I be between jobs without running through our savings?"

"Does it appear as if I can still retire at sixty?"

"How much of a salary cut can I take and still pay my bills and retire on time?"

Josh and Nicole went through each scenario, explaining the options in detail.

Finally, after they reviewed all of the pages in the black leather binder and answered the questions Tom and Lydia proposed, the group fell silent.

"It's one thing to look at the numbers, but it's also essential to look at what your goal really is and then see how those numbers support it," Nicole said.

"This is the live-your-life-differently part, right?" Tom asked, half-joking.

Nicole was first to respond. "Think of it this way," she said. "Why go blindly in one direction, just because that's where you've been headed? Once you define what you'd like to do, say if you do want to retire in ten years and move to Wilmington and lead a leisurely retirement life, does your current financial direction support it?"

Tom shook his head. "I don't think so, no. Not without working longer."

"But is moving to Wilmington really your ultimate goal?" Nicole pressed.

Tom and Lydia looked at her blankly. "Well, yes, that's what we said," Tom replied uncertainly.

"Well, actually, you said you wanted to enjoy your life while you were healthy," Nicole reminded them. "What does that look like? Is that only possible in Wilmington? Is it only possible after retirement?"

Tom and Lydia looked at each other. In their dreams, their ideal life had always started *in the future*. They never considered that it could start now.

"Tom, in the outplacement workshop, I gave you the LifePrinting workbook. Did you and Lydia have a chance to go through it?" Josh asked.

Tom shook his head sheepishly. "I gave it a glance, but I didn't really sit down with it. Or show it to you, Lydia," he admitted to his wife.

"I'm not sure I would have looked at it closely at the time, either," Lydia confessed. "But I'd like to see it now."

"This would be the ideal time," Josh agreed. "Do you still have it handy?"

Tom nodded. "It's on the desk in my home office. Right where I left it that first day!" He smiled ruefully.

"Some of our clients don't initially see the value of this kind of introspection, but when you invest a little time on it, it can provide some incredible insights," Josh said.

"So . . . more homework?" Tom groaned.

"This will be a little more interactive than when you pulled together your financial data," Nicole smiled. "It sounds as though you two are already starting the conversation of what's important to you, and the LifePrinting exercises can help you in that process."

"We'd like for you to bring the workbook to our next meeting," Josh said, "where we'll go through it and see how to best connect your finances with those things that mean the most to you, that motivate you and bring you joy."

"Will it tell me how to find a six-figure job in the next month?" Tom asked, only half joking.

"Uh, no," Josh responded laughingly, "but it can help you determine if you *need* a six-figure job to make you happy."

◎ ◎ ◎ Three months later, Tom hung up the phone in his home office. He had just told Nicole his good news and he was surprised that she was as excited as he was. He shook his head. Who would have thought that he would be almost giddy? This job wasn't the same six-figure senior level position he had imagined he needed. Instead, it was a managerial position at a non-profit organization that helped entrepreneurs grow their startups. The idea of building something, even tangentially, energized Tom in a way that work at Midwest hadn't in years. Here, his age and experience were valued.

That was one of the discoveries he made working through the Life-Printing exercises—how important it was to him, to his sense of self-worth, that what he did was useful, that he could be a hero. He used to think he could only do that by being a company man, but as he and Lydia went through the exercises and he answered a question about finding his meaningful purpose, he had his *ah-ha* moment. *I want to help other people succeed*, Tom thought. At Midwest, Tom had felt immense satisfaction whenever he helped an employee navigate a tough situation. That was part of his job as a manager, but it was one he didn't get to focus on nearly enough. In his new job, he could be a mentor, a guide to help others accomplish their goals. Even better, he would have a reasonable workweek, not the usual sixty-hour Midwest one. How great was that?

Before he started working with Allworth Financial, Tom wouldn't have even considered a salary cut, let alone a move into the non-profit sector. "How much money do you really need to live and to be happy?" Josh and Nicole had asked him repeatedly in that follow-up meeting to review the LifePrinting exercises and examine their financial direction.

"I'm not happy now, so obviously, I need more!" Tom shot back irritably.

Lydia looked at him in stunned surprise. "Where did that come from?"

"I'm not really unhappy, but I guess I'm not happy, either," Tom said. "I'm bound by financial obligations that I can't control."

"Like your children's college tuition?" Nicole asked.

"Yes. And the mortgage. And the property taxes and car payments. It's not like I can just stop paying those."

"Why not?" Lydia asked.

"What?" Tom looked at his wife.

"Well, we don't have to have the mortgage," Lydia said, tentatively at first and then gaining steam. "We bought that house when the kids were still living at home, but they're not likely to come back to live with us after college. Why do we need such a big place?"

"But you love that house!" Tom protested.

"I *did* love it," Lydia said. "But now, with the kids gone, it's really too big, Tom. I didn't want to say anything to disappoint you, but I wouldn't mind something smaller, with less upkeep."

Nicole and Josh smiled at the couple. This was the kind of breakthrough they loved to see. Not only were Lydia and Tom being honest with each other, but also they were thinking creatively about how to get to their goal.

"Let's look at what the sale of your home would do for you financially," Nicole suggested.

As Tom realized that the barriers and obligations he had assumed were insurmountable were not, he turned to Lydia. "Hon, let's not wait until we're retired to be happy, to live our lives."

Lydia felt a quick surge of happiness as she looked at her husband, who suddenly reminded her very much of the handsome young college man she had once known.

"Agreed."

Josh and Nicole showed the Jensons how much money they would need to retire comfortably and used those figures to determine how much Tom needed to earn. To Tom's surprise, once the value of the house was estimated, the amount needed was less than he had assumed.

"Is there a way to put aside money in case Laura wants to go to grad school?" Tom asked.

Josh and Nicole looked at the Jensons' investments and taxes and suggested several changes that would allow them to develop an education fund. It might not fund a complete grad school program, but it would give her a head start.

"It may be a little selfish on my part, but it wouldn't be the end of the world if she had to earn some of her tuition," Tom said.

"We don't even know if she'll go to grad school anyway," Lydia reminded him.

"This is quite a different mindset from the one you had in our initial meeting," Josh remarked. He loved facilitating conversations that might be hard to have but that ultimately helped clients reach the best conclusion on their own.

"I think I spent so much time being a company man and a family man that this downsizing actually gave me permission to figure out what *I* need," Tom said.

Now, after telling Nicole about his new managerial job at the nonprofit, Tom hung up the phone and stood in the hallway for a moment, thinking about all of the recent changes. Several days after that meeting with Josh and Nicole, Lydia had announced that she was going to get a job.

"But why?" Tom asked. They were in the backyard, pulling weeds and trimming the hedges in preparation for an open house the next day.

"I realized that I want to do something I'll enjoy and that also earns a paycheck," she explained. "Even if it's not much compared to your salary, that income will help us get to retirement."

Sure enough, two weeks later, Lydia was the new secretary at the local preschool, where she was having a blast. Little dreams, indeed.

Tom glanced at his watch and knew he'd better go. He was picking Lydia up from work so they could go to dinner at a funky Thai place that had just opened—they'd be celebrating his new job.

As he closed his front door behind him and headed to his car, he nodded at the "Sold" sign on his front lawn. Changes were coming, but this time, they didn't bring fear. They brought anticipation . . . perhaps even excitement.

RETIREMENT PLANNING: ADVICE FROM JOSH AND NICOLE

When people leave one job, particularly when it's not a voluntary decision, they often rush to replace that job with an identical one. But once Tom realized he had the financial breathing room to allow him time to think, he could consider what his ideal work environment looked like. He assumed it would be another corporate environment but realized that

the true inspiration he sought was to feel that he was making a difference. That type of work brought an improvement to his overall quality
of life, and once he determined how his finances could work with his new
venture, he began to look forward to his future.

We often ask our clients key questions to help them identify their
essentials for happiness.

1. What does your ideal work environment look like?
2. What are your core values?
3. What are you passionate about?
4. If you only had six months to live, how would you fill your days?

Answering these questions, with an advisor or even on your own, can
help you determine what is most important in your next career move.

QUESTIONS TO CONSIDER DURING TRANSITION

1. What is your minimum income requirement?
   - How much do you spend each month to live your life?
   - How much did you save monthly into retirement plans, college
     savings, etc.?
2. Do you want to change careers?
3. Do you want to start your own business?
4. What do you do with your health insurance?
   - COBRA vs. individual plan
5. How do you handle your old employer 401(k) or pension plan?
6. Do you have a severance package?
7. Have you reviewed your separation package?
8. What is your ideal work environment?
9. If you could do anything, what would it be?

CHAPTER 6

NAVIGATING THE WRONG TURN
CLIENT STORY: ETHAN AND DEANNA LEWIS

"IT'S NOT GETTING WHAT YOU WANT.
IT'S WANTING WHAT YOU'VE GOT."
Sheryl Crow, Singer/Songwriter

Ethan Lewis glanced at his wife Deanna as she unbuckled her seat belt. She was quiet, not so much in response to the upcoming meeting at Allworth Financial but because of the emotional conversation with their daughter that morning.

"She wants to come home, but I told her not to," Deanna said, feeling her husband's worried eyes on her. She looked up and gave Ethan a brief smile. "Really. It's just a biopsy. There's no need to leave school and come home for that. If—if it's more serious, we can talk about it then."

Ethan nodded and unbuckled his own seat belt, opened his car door, and stepped out. God! His chest felt tight, and even when he tried to take a deep breath, It wasn't enough to calm his nerves. He had thought the worst had happened a few weeks ago when he found out that the biotechnology company he worked for was being sold. Absorbed, really, which meant that the bigger company wanted his company's technology and maybe a few of their senior scientists but not people like Ethan. The bigger company had enough staff with business planning experience already.

Ethan had seen the writing on the wall. Hell, it was a smart business move for advancing his company's technology; with the larger company, more research dollars could be invested. But for the other executives and for junior level scientists and engineers, the news wasn't as good. Ethan had put out a few feelers as soon as what he called his "Spidey sense" started tingling—that Spider-Man-like intuitive power that told him something was wrong. There was little response to his feelers so far, but Ethan hadn't been extremely worried yet. The company severance plan had been generous, and Ethan was sure he would find a similar job within a few months.

But a few weeks later—on a Monday evening—everything changed. His wife, Deanna, had walked into the family room and said six simple words: "I need to talk to you."

"Sure, hon. What?" Ethan asked, never taking his eyes off Monday Night Football. It took him a few moments to register that Deanna didn't answer, but finally, when the commercial break began, he looked at her. His stomach clenched as she furtively wiped away tears. She never liked him to see her cry.

"Deanna, what is it?" he asked, picking up the remote and turning off the television.

"I think it's back, Ethan. The cancer is back," she said, then began crying in earnest, too distraught to even care that Ethan was looking.

Six years ago, Deanna had found a lump in her right breast. A biopsy confirmed it was early stage breast cancer, but fortunately, subsequent tests indicated that the small mass was contained. Deanna had surgery to remove the lump and underwent several rounds of chemo. At the end, her tests were clean, and she went back regularly for follow-up scans. Until now, she and Ethan felt they had dodged a bullet.

"What do you mean, it's back?" Ethan asked, trying to sound calm. Deanna wiped her face with her hands, tucked her wavy brown hair behind her ears, and sighed.

"I went for my mammogram last week, and the radiologist called me today. They saw something abnormal and want me to come back in for another reading," Deanna said.

"Maybe it's not cancer, Dee. Mammograms don't always take great pictures. Maybe they just need a clearer picture," Ethan ventured.

But the second mammogram was just as troubling, and Deanna's doctor scheduled her for a biopsy. Deanna thought the waiting would be the hard part, but breaking the news to the kids was far harder. Samantha, now a freshman at the University of Wisconsin, was thirteen years old when Deanna first got sick. Samantha had always been particularly close to Deanna, and the idea that her mother could be sick again was crushing. That was one reason Samantha opted to go to school close to home. Jake, their fifteen-year-old, was nine when Deanna first battled cancer, and his memories were fuzzy about that time, except for remembering that Grandma, Deanna's mom, stayed with them for a month.

Now, Deanna and Ethan both stood on opposite sides of the car, facing the two-story white building across the small parking lot.

"Are you sure you want to do this?" Ethan asked as he rounded the car and took Deanna's hand.

"We can't put it off," she replied, giving his hand a squeeze. "We put together a ton of information, and we need to figure out our financial situation, no matter what happens."

"Nothing bad will happen," Ethan said, more fiercely than he intended. "I promise."

Deanna smiled, even though she knew that despite Ethan's assurance, he couldn't make sure everything would be okay. But one thing they could do was go to this meeting.

Wealth managers—or Life Transition Specialists as they were called at Allworth Financial—had made a presentation at one of Ethan's outplacement meetings. Ethan listened attentively as one of the partners, Josh Kadish, talked about the importance of clients truly being happy, as well as educated on their current situation. The offer of a second opinion on he and Deanna's current course was just what the doctor ordered—no pun intended. Ethan had a general idea of their finances, but he wasn't completely clear that they were on track to hit their goals. He was also unsure of how the insurance and estate planning they'd put in place years ago measured up today. Now, with the severance package, he had some important decisions to make about how he would budget and where he would put his funds—and with Deanna's health issue, maintaining health insurance and creating additional savings for out-of-pocket expenses was even more essential.

When Ethan and Deanna opened the door to Allworth Financial, the smell of warm, sweet chocolate enveloped them. Ethan's stomach grumbled and Deanna suppressed a laugh.

"Oh, look, sweetie!" Deanna nudged Ethan as she looked up above the receptionist's desk. A fifty-inch plasma screen proclaimed, "Welcome, Ethan and Deanna Lewis."

"That's nice," Deanna said, smiling.

"Hi, you must be Mr. and Mrs. Lewis?" A young and energetic dark-haired girl looked up from her desk to welcome them.

"Yes. Ethan and Deanna. We have an appointment with Josh Kadish and Nicole Mayer," Ethan said.

"Of course! Welcome to Allworth Financial. I'm Beth and I'll get you settled in the conference room." Beth scooted around the reception desk and led Ethan and Deanna down a short hallway and through an open door into a small conference room. There she offered them their choice of fresh fruit, trail mix, wrapped chocolate candies, and the pièce de résistance—an assortment of warm, freshly baked cookies. "We also have sodas, waters, teas, and coffees."

"It all looks so nice. I'll have a bottled water and Ethan will have a diet soda." Deanna wasn't trying to be bossy; she just always knew what Ethan wanted before he could even say it. That was just one of her small ways of taking care of him.

"Great. I'll be right back with that, and Josh and Nicole will join you in just a minute," Beth said, shutting the door softly behind her.

"Well, nice place," Deanna remarked.

"Yes. So far," Ethan agreed, sitting down and opening up a manila folder he had brought with him. "They seemed thorough in their questions."

When Ethan had called Allworth Financial to schedule an appointment after the initial outplacement presentation, Josh emailed Ethan about what to expect from the meeting, as well as sending some items to complete in advance. Ethan had thought he had a good idea of all of his accounts, but man, when he had to list them all, it was almost like a treasure hunt. He pulled one statement from his old 401(k), two statements from IRA accounts at one brokerage firm, three statements from another, and two more from yet a third. On top of that, he found three life insurance policies and their old will from fifteen years ago, right after Jake was born.

"Hello!" Josh said enthusiastically as he and his partner, Nicole, came in and shook hands with the couple. "Ethan, it's good to see you again.

And, Deanna, so very nice to meet you. How are you two doing?"

Deanna and Ethan looked at each other awkwardly. Nicole glanced at Josh questioningly.

"We're glad you made it to see us," Nicole continued smoothly, with sincere enthusiasm. "Beth should be back in just a minute—oh, here she is," she said as Beth came in with Deanna's bottle of sparkling water and a cute little glass bottle of soda for Ethan. "Thanks, Beth," Nicole said. Beth nodded briskly and left the room, once again closing the door softly as she left.

After a few minutes of small talk, Josh turned to the business at hand. "So, Ethan, when you and I talked on the phone, you said you wanted to make sure you understood your total financial picture so you could plan for a potential period of unemployment. You were also receiving a severance package and wanted to know how to position that for the interim and long-term security."

Josh waited while Ethan nodded in agreement.

"Has anything changed since then?" Josh, too, had noticed the change in mood in the couple earlier and wanted to address the elephant in the room.

Ethan opened his mouth and closed it.

Deanna sat up in her seat. "Well, I'm undergoing some medical tests, and we're not quite sure how they'll turn out." Her voice was strong, but she couldn't help the slight quiver in the corner of her mouth. "I'm going to have to have a biopsy."

"That waiting is so hard." Nicole reached out and put a reassuring hand on Deanna's arm. "I'm so sorry you have to go through this."

Even if the results weren't life threatening, Nicole knew the time spent waiting for an answer could feel like eons. She had experienced a serious health scare herself a few years ago when doctors found a tumor on her liver. The nurses initially told her that most tumors like hers were benign, but she couldn't sleep until she got the biopsy results. In those lonely dark hours, she wondered, *What if?* What if she died soon, leaving little Gavin without a mom? What if she lived but spent years in a downward health spiral? What if her condition was treatable, but she spent months undergoing chemotherapy or some debilitating medical treatment? What would happen to her son? Her job? Her life? After surgery to remove one-third of her liver, Nicole was now healthy, but she vowed never to forget that period of uncertainty or take her health for granted.

Looking at Deanna, Nicole sent up a prayer of gratitude once more for her own positive outcome, as well as a request for Deanna to have the same results. In the meantime, she might not be able to help Deanna medically, but she could definitely help her become more educated and aware financially.

"We'll get through it," Ethan said, wanting to stay focused.

"Why don't we take a look at the information you brought in?" Josh suggested.

"We should consider, of course, how Deanna's health affects some of the ideas we initially discussed. Have you considered whether your job search strategies will change, depending on how she is doing?"

Ethan blinked. He hadn't thought that far ahead. "I don't know. I mean, I assumed I would find a similar job, here in the area, with a similar salary. A good health insurance plan is important."

"Do you have your severance agreement with you?" Nicole asked. Her brow knitted, and she felt the familiar tingle of beginning the detective work. Ethan and Deanna were presenting them with a puzzle, and this is where they started forming an idea of what the final picture might look like. "What does it provide for health insurance?"

Ethan shifted through some papers. "It gives me six months of coverage, with the option of signing up for COBRA afterward. I just assumed that in six months, I would have another job. COBRA is expensive, but with the kids and Deanna, we can't do without health insurance."

"That makes absolute sense," Josh said. "Have you signed these papers yet?"

Ethan shook his head.

Josh thought about it. Most people assumed they would find comparable jobs within six months, but the reality was often surprising. And if that were the case here, Ethan and Deanna would be left in a terrible lurch. "Is there an opportunity for you to negotiate for say, a year of benefits before COBRA kicks in?" Josh asked.

"I don't know. I hadn't thought about it. I can check," Ethan said, writing a note on pad of paper.

"That's a good idea," Nicole said. "As we talk about your total financial picture, we can also look at your health insurance, your life insurance, your investments, your estate planning documents, and anything else you can think of. We will also look at your obligations, such as your son's and daughter's tuition, your mortgage, car payments, taxes, and other expenses to help you see exactly how much money you have to work with."

"That sounds good," Ethan said, though he felt slightly overwhelmed.

Josh saw the glance Ethan and Deanna exchanged and understood: this couple, like so many he and Nicole saw, had worked hard and planned carefully to create a comfortable, sustainable lifestyle for their family. But like most people, after awhile, they went on autopilot. Regular payments came in and went out, health insurance plans were quickly renewed, and investments were largely left alone. This was simply what happened in the course of actually living life, and it wasn't until crisis—or, in the Lewises' case, *crises*—hit that the larger picture came into view again. Josh knew that the concept of looking at everything together could be daunting, but he and Nicole fervently believed in its necessity.

"One of our fundamental beliefs is that our clients should be educated about where they are today and where they want to go tomorrow. That way, they're in a position to make decisions moving forward with confidence," Josh said. "We have some exercises we'd encourage you to go through that will help." Josh handed Ethan and Deanna a folder. "This is our LifePrinting workbook, and it helps our clients define and prioritize what is most important in their lives. We find that when they do this, it gives them the clarity to make better life and financial decisions."

"If you are up to it, why don't the two of you read through it together and see how you might answer some of these questions?" Nicole suggested. "It's a great way of making sure that you're both on the same page as you navigate these transitions. When we meet again, we can see how that may point us in the right direction for you and your family."

"We'll do that," Deanna said, patting the folder. It would be a great idea to make sure that she and Ethan were both singing from the same song sheet as they prepared to move forward with whatever life might throw at them.

"For now, let's go through the information you brought in today," Josh said.

❯❯❯ Most follow-up appointments occurred sooner than eight weeks out, but with Deanna's surgery and follow-up chemotherapy, this was the first week she felt well enough to schedule a meeting. When Ethan suggested that he come in without her, Josh and Nicole suggested that they wait until both he and Deanna could be there; Josh and Nicole were happy to accommodate the Lewises' schedule.

Greeting Ethan and Deanna in the conference room the second time, Josh and Nicole couldn't help but notice that Deanna looked much more fragile than before. Her shoulders came to sharp peaks beneath her floral silk blouse, and she moved carefully and deliberately, as if not completely trusting her body. Ethan didn't look much better. He had lost ten pounds, and he had a constant wrinkle in his forehead, as if from permanent worry.

"How are you doing?" Nicole sat down next to Deanna as Josh went to talk to Ethan. "I mean, really," she added gently. "How are you doing?"

So many people asked her how she was doing, Deanna thought. But they didn't really want to hear the details. There was something in Nicole's blue eyes, though—the way she looked right at Deanna without being uncomfortable—that made Deanna want to talk.

"There are days and there are days," Deanna said in a tired half-whisper. "Sometimes, I'm just so angry, you know? We went through this before. No need for a mastectomy, my doctor said back then. A lumpectomy would take care of it. This time, I told the surgeon, take it all. Take the other one, too. I do not want to deal with this again," she said forcefully. Then she sighed, tears welling up in her eyes. "But I am so tired."

Ethan caught the tail end of the conversation and interrupted his discussion with Josh. "Babe, you went from surgery to chemo so fast, you haven't had a chance to recover. You'll get there. Just be gentle with yourself, remember?"

Deanna offered Ethan a small smile, and as Nicole watched the couple interact, she felt a surge of warmth for them both. It was no easier to watch helplessly as your partner suffered than to be the one in pain—she knew.

Indeed, Ethan felt as though he were sleeping with one eye open and one ear always cocked to hear if Deanna made a sound. As much as this latest health crisis had shaken her, it may have shaken him even more. When she received her previous diagnosis, maybe being busy at work kept Ethan anchored. He could almost ignore the fear by delving into his job. This time, he didn't have anywhere to hide. But he rose to the occasion. He went with Deanna to all of her appointments, asking insightful questions and taking notes, which was particularly helpful when Deanna occasionally found herself in a vortex of emotion as the doctors explained test results and next steps. He made special time to take their son, Jake, out for lunch or movies or just to hang—something he had not done before. One weekend, while Deanna's mother was staying with them as Deanna continued her recovery from surgery, Ethan drove up to University of Wisconsin for Parents' Weekend, treating Samantha and her roommate to an expensive steak dinner. Deanna and Ethan had discouraged Samantha from coming home for Deanna's surgery, preferring that she concentrate on her studies, but Ethan knew his daughter also needed a little love from home.

"It's certainly okay if you say no, but did you have a chance to review the exercises in the LifePrinting workbook or to think about your primary goals?" Josh said, drawing everyone's attention back to the topic at hand.

"Yeah, I did. We did," Ethan corrected himself. He had brought the workbook to look at while he sat next to Deanna's bed after she returned from surgery. The oncologist had met with him, saying that he was very pleased with the outcome of the surgery. It was the aggressive double mastectomy approach Deanna had wanted, but added that with her previous medical history, it was the right decision. Ethan shuddered now, recalling his wife looking so pale and still on the bed. If he lost her, he didn't know what he would do. How he would even put one foot in front of the other?

"I know I had talked about finding a new job, same as the old one, same status as the old one, same salary as the old one," Ethan began. "Salary is important, but some things are more essential." He leaned forward in his chair. "Deanna's doing better. The doctors are encouraged that she will make a full recovery. And we're praying for that every day. But this has taught me, taught us, that the future isn't a given."

"I could get sick again," Deanna added. "Not that I'm planning to. Or Ethan could get hit by a car. We don't have unlimited time. Or energy. Or health."

"We need to make space for what's important," Ethan continued. "And that's our family. Whatever time we have, we want to make the most of it."

Josh smiled. This was what he and Nicole lived for—helping people who truly understood what was essential in life and making those things a priority.

"It sounds like you've been doing a lot of thinking," Josh said. "How does this translate into what you want to do with your next job and your finances?"

"Well, I want to work. I have to work," Ethan said, "for financial reasons and healthcare as well as for my own enjoyment. But I don't need to work the crazy and unpredictable hours I used to. I want to have dinner with Dee, at least most nights. I want to go to Jake's school events. I want us to go on family vacations, not necessarily huge ones once a year, but maybe a getaway once a month without worrying that the work will be piled mountain high when I get back. I want to go to any doctor's appointments with Deanna without getting back to work and feeling that I've shirked my duty. So I want to work, but I also want a life," he concluded.

"That gives us a great picture of what you're looking for," Nicole said. "Have you worked with the career counselor your company suggested?"

"I did at the beginning, but back then I was looking for just another high-powered job. Then Dee had surgery, and I put everything on hold. Now, I'm looking for something different, and I have an appointment to talk with the counselor about my new goals. I'm feeling very positive about them," Ethan said.

Nicole nodded. "That's excellent, Ethan. You've obviously done a lot of soul searching these last few months."

"I have, and it's been worth it."

"Deanna, what about you? Has your perspective changed on what direction you'd like your family to take?" Nicole asked.

Deanna shrugged. "I don't know. I really don't. You know, it's funny. We thought it was such bad timing that he lost his job at the same time my cancer returned. But actually, it was a gift. He had time to be with me and help me get through this. That wouldn't have happened if he had been working. So while he doesn't need to be around *all* of the time," she gave Ethan a wry grin that spoke of her old sense of humor, "I do want him home in the evenings and on weekends. Like he said, I want him to spend time with the kids because they have very little time left to be in our house. Sam still considers our house home, but in four years, she'll be ready for something new. And in a few years, Jake will be off to college. We don't have a lot of time to all be together, and I want to make the most of it."

Nicole nodded, and in the comfortable silence that followed, Deanna continued.

"I guess I'd most like time to recover. Time to get strong. Help to get more fit, maybe with a personal trainer. Someone to run errands and just make my life a little easier so I can spend some time getting back to being me," she said. "I don't have big goals. I just want to be healthy and have my family."

"Those are excellent goals to have," Josh said. "Now that we know what you'd like your life to look like, let's talk about how to accomplish that."

Nothing was guaranteed, Deanna thought as she watched Josh and Nicole outline financial options. The folks at Allworth Financial couldn't guarantee the cancer wouldn't come back. Ethan, for all of his vigilance, couldn't fight against cells within her body. Ethan looked at his wife, and she smiled, putting a hand on his arm. Maybe the trick wasn't to figure out how to have more time or more money. Maybe the trick was to find fulfillment with whatever time or money you had.

PREPARING FINANCES DURING OR AFTER AN ILLNESS: ADVICE FROM JOSH AND NICOLE

Ethan's and Deanna's situation was a difficult one. No one wants to think about serious illness or the possibility of death, particularly at a young age. But Deanna's illness forced the couple to take a hard look at what mattered. With a very real concern that their time left together may be short, Ethan and Deanna could focus on how they wanted their lives to matter, to each other, to their children, and to others in the world.

With health coverage a particular concern, Ethan and Deanna needed to understand their options clearly, particularly for maintaining continued coverage. Health coverage might be one of the major benefits that Ethan looked for in his next job, focusing on companies and industries that had generous coverage.

Although Ethan and Deanna faced an uncertain future, the truth is, all of us do. Illness or accidents can change our lives in an instant. That's not intended to be discouraging, but more to emphasize the need for creating a compelling vision of how we want to live. We encourage our clients to consider other key questions such as what would they pursue if they weren't afraid, what would make their lives feel complete and how they want to be remembered.

Ethan and Deanna realized that while they needed money to pay for medical treatment, for their home, and for their everyday life, the legacy that they established with their family was more important.

Instead of needing a job similar to what he already had, Ethan realized that with his renewed desire to be fully involved with his wife and children, he needed a job that offered more balance, not necessarily more money. Once Ethan and Deanna understood their finances and their options, they were better equipped to create their future, for whatever length of time that was.

When we talk with clients who face life-threatening illnesses, we caution them against making decisions too quickly. We don't want them to become paralyzed by fear, so we walk them through steps one at a time. Doing that lets them put systems in place to make life flow smoothly for whoever is handling finances. Establishing online bill paying, ensuring both spouses or responsible family members know where important financial information is stored, using Allworth Financials' *LifePrint Navigator*, and making sure clients are better educated about their big picture are some of the ways we help clients feel more in control, even when their world has been shaken.

QUICK TIPS

1. Review your current healthcare coverage.
2. Make sure your wills and trusts are up to date.
3. Have one single place with all pertinent information.
   - Include who to call in event of emergency (financial planner, attorney, CPA, doctors).

- Include where to find your most current wills/trusts/durable powers of attorney for property and healthcare.
4. How do you want to be remembered?
    - Write your own eulogy and identify what needs to change in order for others to remember you that way.

CHAPTER 7

STARTING AGAIN
CLIENT STORY: PATRICIA FELTON

"DON'T CRY BECAUSE IT'S OVER, SMILE BECAUSE IT HAPPENED."
Dr. Seuss, Author, *Green Eggs and Ham*

No one gets married to get divorced! There is such hope, promise, excitement, and love in the process and institution of marriage that the D word is whispered, shunned, and generally not spoken about in the presence of newlyweds.

Patricia sat at the conference table, replaying the conversation from the night before. Her soon-to-be ex-husband, Greg, was carrying on that she was wasting money on the attorney she hired to represent her. "Why can't you just be reasonable?" he asked. She smiled as she relived her reply: "I'm perfectly willing to be reasonable. Hiring a good attorney just helps assure me that you are."

She took a bite of the still-warm, freshly baked chocolate chip cookie on the table in front of her. Dang, these were good! Who would have thought that she would actually look forward to these meetings? But the virtual and literal handholding at Allworth Financial had made sessions there one of the infrequent bright spots in her "new" life. Patricia glanced down at her left hand, still startled by the bare band of skin on her ring finger. She had taken her wedding ring off a few weeks ago, no longer holding on to false hope that her marriage could be saved.

"Hi, Patricia." Nicole Mayer walked into the conference room with her usual bright smile.

Patricia pasted on an answering smile as she rose to shake Nicole's hand. For a moment, she felt a flash of envy. Today and in their first meeting a month ago, Nicole looked completely put together: chic blond hair perfectly coiffed, bold beaded necklace brightening her face. And Nicole *knew* stuff. She could rattle off financial details that Patricia could only barely grasp. And yet, Nicole always noticed when Patricia's eyes began to glaze over, and she stopped for a break before going back over the information at a slower pace.

"Good morning, Patricia." Josh Kadish, Nicole's partner, strode into the room, closing the door behind him. "Nice to see you. How are you this morning?"

"Fine, thanks," Patricia replied. She was always a little awkward at the beginning of meetings, despite Nicole and Josh's warmth. Greg used to say her shyness was charming. Now, he just thought it gave him license to try to intimidate her during their divorce proceedings. Patricia sighed. To be fair, she used to love the way Greg took charge. Now, she thought of it as him trying to take over. Divorce can definitely change one's perspective of an ex-spouse's qualities.

Nicole sat down next to Patricia. "How are your girls?"

"They're doing really well." Patricia gave a genuine smile as she thought about her daughters. "Jamie is busy being a pre-teen, with all its drama, but she's adjusting to middle school. Lilly is great. She loves her teacher and is clamoring to get a puppy. As if we needed more chaos!" Patricia laughed. "And Jaden," her voice softened. "She's at that stage where, at five, she's not too big to sit in my lap. I know how quickly that stage can pass, so I'm not rushing her one bit!"

Nicole laughed. Her son, Gavin, was four, and he seemed to have grown a little each morning when he climbed out from beneath his Spider-Man covers. Nicole looked at Patricia carefully. She could see the strain of the divorce on Patricia's face. Now divorced as well, Nicole knew about trying to put on a brave face for the children, for the world. But here, in the Allworth Financial offices, Nicole wanted Patricia to be at ease. She didn't have to pretend in front of them.

"And how are *you?*" Nicole asked gently.

"Don't ask me that!" Patricia said, half laughing even as tears pricked her eyes. Josh nudged a box of tissues closer as he sat down at the table.

"Greg called last night. He didn't like the settlement offer my attorney sent over, so Greg was yelling at me that I was greedy and that I wasn't being realistic. He said that when the girls would need something, he was just going to tell them that he couldn't afford it because Mommy was taking all the money!" Patricia reached for a tissue and dabbed the corners of her eyes. "And this was the man I was married to for fourteen years. Can you believe that?" She sighed. "Sometimes I think it would be better if I just said, sure, whatever you want, Greg. If I just signed the damned papers and finished this thing. I can't take it anymore."

"That can seem like the easiest way," Nicole said gently. "But is it the best way? Emotions naturally run high for both parties in a divorce, but it's important to focus on making the best decisions. Not just for you, but for your girls, especially down the road."

"Patricia, we know this is difficult on so many levels," Josh added. "Not only are you handling the dissolution of your marriage, but you're also negotiating custody and finances. It gets messy and uncomfortable, and it may seem that if you give up what you want to make Greg happy, things will go more smoothly."

"I'm just so tired of all the fighting," Patricia said. She hated the resigned, begging tone in her voice, knowing that on some level she was asking for permission to quit.

"Let me ask you this," Nicole said. "You and Greg were married for quite some time. I'm sure that, like all couples, you had disagreements along the way."

Patricia's eyes flashed as she recalled past arguments. "Absolutely."

"How did those arguments get resolved?" Nicole asked.

Patricia thought a moment and then sighed. "I usually did what Greg wanted, just to keep the peace. Like when we moved last year. The girls and I were happy in Vernon Hills. We had a great house, friendly neighbors, and a good school. But Greg wanted to move closer to where he was raised, so we moved to a new neighborhood where everyone is in cliques. The girls were miserable and so was I, but Greg liked being able to say that he was able to afford that neighborhood and be back where he grew up."

"Would you say that filing for divorce is one of the first times you haven't done what Greg wanted?" Nicole asked.

"Probably. I don't know why he didn't want a divorce. He didn't act as if he wanted our marriage!" Patricia said bitterly. "Maybe because I insisted on it after I realized that even after I forgave him for his affair last year, it was still going on."

"And, in addition to insisting on the divorce," Nicole pressed, "you're now telling Greg how much money you feel is fair for you to have as part of the settlement. That's another example of you doing what's best for you, instead of just going along with what's easiest."

Patricia thought a moment about what Nicole said. The way she phrased it, it sounded so justified, not as though she was a gold digger.

"That brings us to the topic of today's meeting," Josh said, easing into the transition. "Last time we met, we advised you to make a list of your monthly expenditures. We want to start looking at a long-term settlement for you when the divorce is final and not just this temporary arrangement during the separation."

Patricia dug into her handbag and pulled out a folder filled with papers. "I brought you everything I could find."

In her initial meeting with Allworth Financial, Patricia walked in not knowing what to expect. Her divorce attorney had recommended that she talk with Allworth Financial to help understand the financial side of the divorce, which would help them determine where to start negotiating the divorce settlement. During that first meeting, Patricia began to realize just how much she didn't know. How much money did Greg make in a year, counting bonuses? Where were their investments? What tax decisions had they made that had long-term implications? Even questions like how much they spent on groceries, clothes, restaurants, and entertainment stumped her. Although Patricia had worked until her youngest child was born, her salary was a fraction of what Greg made, and she had blindly used the platinum Amex card whenever she or the girls needed—or wanted—something, not thinking of how much it cost. Now Greg had cancelled the card, along with their membership to the gym and the country club, and told her she had to trade in her big SUV for a smaller, more economical car.

"Look, I'm paying for the house plus my apartment," Greg had said. "I can only afford so much, Patricia. It's only going to get worse."

And Patricia realized she had no response. It seemed that Greg always had plenty of money, but now he was acting as if this divorce was going to send them to the poor house. He had always handled their finances, making the major investment decisions. At the time, Patricia hadn't minded because she trusted him. But now, she didn't know if she should believe anything he said, even when he claimed to be trying to help.

"How was it, gathering all of this information?" Josh asked as he began looking through the folder.

"It was awful! I hate those details," Patricia confessed. "I did like you suggested and went through my previous bank statements and credit card bills to categorize my spending. I have to admit, I was shocked at how much we spend on incidentals. Lunches out. Dinners on the go after the kids' dance class or piano lessons. Satellite television with all the movie channels. Even Jamie's cell phone bill adds up over the course of the year. Greg insisted on getting her an iPhone when she started middle school. What kid needs an iPhone in middle school?

"But anyway, we spend a lot of money, probably on a lot of things we don't need. It's our life, what we've gotten used to. It's hard to cut down. I don't want to be the one to tell my daughter I'm taking away her iPhone!" Patricia said.

"I know kids and their phones," Josh concurred. "My kids would feel completely deprived if they didn't have the cool phones their friends did. And as we strategize for your budget, we do need to prioritize what's most important, especially among the non-essentials. For you and your girls, having phones may be critical. Do they have to be smart phones? Maybe, maybe not. Do they have to be iPhones? Maybe, maybe not. Do you have the phone plan that gives you the best rates? That could make a difference between something being affordable and something being more of an indulgence."

Patricia thought about that for a minute. "I never considered things like phone plans as something that could be changed."

"That's just one example," Nicole said. "Budgeting is not just about cutting things out. It's about becoming more efficient and prioritizing, but it's also making way for the things you really want. Another example—we can look at your taxes and see if there are different investment directions that can actually help you keep more of what you make and give less to Uncle Sam.

"I know this is hard, Patricia," Nicole continued. "But you have to remember that you have options. We can help you figure out what they are. And not only do you have options, but you also have a responsibility. You have to make sure you and your girls have what you need, no matter what Greg tries to pull. It's up to you now to make sure your daughters' financial futures are secure."

"So in other words, I have to put on my big girl panties, huh?" Patricia said ruefully. She took a deep breath. "Okay. Let's get started."

Page by page, Nicole and Josh went over the financial story of her life, asking for details on expenses, discussing options, and developing a draft budget for child support and alimony.

After about an hour, Josh leaned back and stretched his arms. "I think this is a solid budget for your lawyer to work with," he said. "We've thought about what your girls may need one, three, five, and ten years down the road. We've included a college fund for each child, and we've allowed time and educational funds for you to re-train and begin a new career."

Patricia rubbed her eyes tiredly. "It makes sense, and I can see how it all fits together, but what happens if Greg doesn't agree? No matter what I propose, he'll object. He'll say I'm asking for too much."

"What do you think, Patricia?" Nicole asked. "Do you think you're asking for too much?"

"No! Not at all. These items we have listed—they're not just whims. We've put a lot of thought into exactly what we need," Patricia responded. "We started with the guideline settlement numbers you said are common in Illinois for maintenance and child support, and then based our figures on true projections of our future needs."

Nicole smiled with satisfaction, proud of her student. "And that's exactly what you and your lawyer should tell Greg. You now understand what you need and why. It's not being greedy. It's not being selfish. It's being realistic."

"And looking out for my girls," Patricia added.

"And protecting your own future," Josh chimed in. "There's nothing wrong with that. Once the settlement is finalized, we can then work with you on how you'll handle that—investments, possible sale of the house, or whatever you'd like to do."

Nicole and Josh looked at Patricia as she processed all of the information she had absorbed in the meeting. The lines of strain were still there, but Patricia sat a little straighter in her chair and spoke a little more firmly, with increasing confidence.

"You get one bite of the apple, so you have to make sure it's the right amount for you to chew," Josh reminded her. "Too little and you'll be hungry, and it's not easy to go back and get more than you initially settled for."

Patricia nodded. "I can do this. I know why we came up with this budget. I know what I'm entitled to, and I shouldn't let Greg bully me into accepting less than what is fair. To be honest, I know this has to be hard on him, too. I don't care all that much that it is, but I do understand that some his behavior is because he's hurt—just like some of my behavior is because I am hurt.

"But I think that now I can separate the financial piece from that and talk about it logically, without feeling that I'll get taken advantage of," Patricia said. She shook her head, adding quietly, "It's so sad, though. I never imagined that I would be divorced."

"You'll get through it," Nicole said.

"Promise?" Patricia asked, only half kiddingly.

Nicole nodded firmly. "I promise. When Ken and I divorced, it was the hardest thing I'd ever done. I wondered if I was doing the right thing. I wondered how it would affect my son. But ultimately, I also realized this represented a new start for me—a necessary new start. It was a new start for Ken, too. And we're better apart than we were together."

"I don't think my relationship with Greg will ever be better," Patricia said.

"Once the emotion of the divorce and the settlement is over, it often gets easier. And it's important to try, for your girls' sake," Nicole said. "But that doesn't mean that you let him steamroll you. You now understand what you and the girls need and what you're entitled to by law. Now it's time to start creating your own future."

"You're right," Patricia nodded. "I know you're right. I just have to keep reminding myself that we'll get through this—that the kids will be okay and so will I. Even though my marriage is over, I have three beautiful girls, so I can't be sorry about that. And now, it's time for the next phase of my life." Patricia nodded again, rising from the table. "I'll keep telling myself that. And soon, I hope, I'll truly believe it."

FINANCIAL AND EMOTIONAL PREPARATION FOR DIVORCE: ADVICE FROM JOSH AND NICOLE

Divorce is fraught with emotion, but as much as possible, try to take the emotional part out so you can concentrate on the financial piece. Doing that helps you reach better conclusions that are based on the law and not on revenge. Understanding your financial situation and what you are entitled to can make you feel much more empowered to insist on that amount without feeling guilty.

Each state has guidelines on child support, and you can likely find out what applies to your situation by searching online for your state's child support guidelines. It is also critical to determine how child support and maintenance could be taxed. Knowing what you are eligible for by law can give you a firmer foundation for negotiation. Understanding and taking charge of your budget is a key piece of establishing a feeling of freedom. Using an expense worksheet and budget, you can see clearly how money is spent, where to allocate it, and how much may be needed to support your loved ones' lives and your own.

GENERAL GUIDELINE EXAMPLE

This will vary by state and by your specific situation. Consult a divorce attorney as this is for illustrative purposes only and should not be construed as legal advice.

1. Maintenance is generally 20% of gross income and is taxable to the recipient for life. It is typically reviewed after seven years.
2. Child support is generally 25% of net income and is not taxable to the recipient. It typically ends when children attain the age of 18 unless there are special needs.

For example:

Married for 15 years, 2–3 kids, gross income $200,000/year

Maintenance (gross and taxable to the recipient):
$200,000 × 20% = $40,000/year/12 = **$3,333/month**

Child support (net and not taxable to the recipient):
$200,000 − 40% = $120,000 × 25% = $30,000/year/12 = **$2,500/month**

The guideline would be a total of **$5833/month**.

Expense Worksheet

Income 1: _____

Income 2: _____

Total Income: _____

Total Expenditures: _____

Additional Funds: _____

Tithing and Donations	MONTHLY	ANNUAL
Tithing		
Fast Offerings		
Charity		
TOTAL		
Taxes		
Federal		
State		
Local		
TOTAL		
Housing		
Mortgage / Rent		
Cell Phone		
Cable / Internet		
Maintenance and Repairs		
Utilities		
TOTAL		
Transportation		
Vehicle Payment		
Insurance		
Fuel		
Maintenance		
Licensing		
Other		
TOTAL		

	MONTHLY	ANNUAL
Entertainment		
Dates		
Movies		
Concerts		
Games		
Other		
TOTAL		
Food		
Groceries		
Dining Out		
Fast Food		
Other		
TOTAL		
Personal Care		
Toiletries		
Clothing		
Gym		
Other		
Other		
TOTAL		
Savings		
Investment		
School		
Retirement		
TOTAL		
Loans		
School		
Credit Card		
Other		
TOTAL		

Be sure to take an inventory of:

1. What you have (assets = savings, checking, CDs, investment accounts, IRAs, 401(k)s, deferred compensation and other pension or retirement plans, real estate, kids' college accounts, etc.)

2. What you owe (liabilities = mortgage, student loans, credit card debt, etc.)

DIVORCE TIPS

1. **Seek good advice early on.** Divorce proceedings are like war in most cases. You need to prepare for the battle. Before you even consider filing, consult with at least three attorneys in your area to find out upfront fees, payment arrangement options, etc. Most cities have legal aid societies, and many lawyers offer free thirty-minute consultations. Also, meet with your accountant to understand tax consequences and other issues related to valuation of property, retirement plans, stocks, and other assets.

2. **Consider the timing of your divorce.** If your spouse is due a bonus or raise, wait until it is paid out before filing to avoid any claim that it's not marital property. If you have been in a long-term marriage, stick it out to the ten-year mark. This will help you get more of your spouse's Social Security. Once you decide to get a divorce, file first. There are advantages in a divorce proceeding for the person who files first.

3. **Make yourself indispensable.** Make sure your name is on all bank accounts, investment accounts, deeds of trust, utilities, etc., and that joint signatures are needed. This will prevent your spouse from raiding your bank accounts.

4. **Make copies of all documents** (such as tax returns, bank statements, credit card bills, W-2 forms, mortgage statements, and loan agreements).

5. **Track down the assets.** You need to know where every penny is. This includes bank accounts, stocks, bonds, jewelry, and other assets. In a divorce, each spouse has to disclose all assets, but often individuals are less than forthcoming. Know what is out there because some portion of it is yours.

6. **Protect your credit.** You will need your credit to start your new lifestyle. Don't co-sign for your spouse.

7. **Try to negotiate temporary support payments.** If you and your spouse are able to talk, try to negotiate temporary alimony and child support payments that will tide you over until the divorce is final.

8. **Separate your money.** Take half of the money out of your accounts so that you will have some money to live on and so that your spouse won't beat you to it.

9. **Dust off your resume.** Even though you may be entitled to alimony, it's discretionary and it won't last forever.

10. **Custody is decided by the courts when contested.** It's better to work something out before getting the courts involved. The courts have an obligation to determine who is in the best position to care for the children and what is in the best interest of the children. In most cases, assuming both parents are fit, the court will award joint custody, as the law assumes children need both parents.

11. **Don't put the kids in the middle.** Keep your kids out of it. Don't involve them in the decision to get a divorce or any of the particulars. It's bad for the kids, and it makes you look bad in a custody battle.

12. **Don't alienate your children from your spouse.** Judges hate this, and it's bad for the children.

13. **Child support is mandated by law,** so don't worry: if your spouse has a job, and you have the kids, he or she will pay child support, and it can be garnished from his or her wages.

14. **Document any type of abuse.**

15. **Carefully choose someone in whom to confide.** During the planning stage, keep your discussions limited to one or two people you can trust and who you know won't talk to your spouse.

16. **Don't fall for the hype.** Don't let your spouse convince you that you will end up with nothing or that you will be kicked out of the house. Your spouse doesn't make these decisions; the judge does. Assume half of everything your spouse owns belongs to you.

CHAPTER 8

THE TALK
CLIENT STORY: JEANNIE AND ADAM DICKERSON, AND ED JOHNSON

"IT'S PARADOXICAL THAT THE IDEA OF LIVING A LONG LIFE
APPEALS TO EVERYONE, BUT THE IDEA OF GETTING OLD
DOESN'T APPEAL TO ANYONE."
Andy Rooney, Writer and Commentator, *60 Minutes*

Nicole paused at the doorway of the conference room. She used the few seconds before she entered to get a read on the new clients. Jeannie Dickerson and her husband, Adam, sat next to Jeannie's father, Ed. Nicole watched them for a moment as Jeannie, deep in conversation with Ed, touched his wrist and laughed. Genuine caring, Nicole thought. As Jeannie sat back in her chair, she saw Nicole.

"Hello!" Nicole entered the room with a bright smile. "I'm Nicole Mayer."

"And I'm Josh Kadish," Josh added as he entered the room right behind her.

"Hi. Nicole and I talked over the phone, but it's nice to meet both of you in person. I'm Jeannie. My husband, Adam, and my dad, Ed Johnson."

They exchanged handshakes. Jeannie's hand was small and delicate, but her handshake was firm. Adam's hand was warm and meaty, but he shook hands carefully, as if tempering his strength. Ed's pale, long-fingered hand was cool and dry, as he gave an efficient, one pump shake. Josh had always thought you could tell a good bit about a person by that first handshake. If he were to guess, he would say that Jeannie was all business, Adam was the protector, and Ed maintained a little distance from people until he was comfortable with them.

"Thanks for meeting with us," Jeannie said as they settled back into their seats. "My father is interested in learning more about long-term planning."

Josh nodded, biting back a smile as Jeannie got right down to business.

"My mom passed away three years ago, and Dad lives alone downstate. He was a professor at the university," Jeannie explained. "But he's getting older now, and I worry that he's too far away if he needs help. We have a lovely woman who comes in a few times a week to clean and grocery shop, but what happens if he needs more than that? We want to make sure Dad is always taken care of."

Nicole nodded understandingly and turned to Ed. "Ed, how would you say things are going for you?" Particularly in cases regarding elder care, it is essential to make sure the parents are not coerced into actions that might not be in their best interest. Sometimes the scent of money makes people do strange things.

"Well, I do all right," Ed said. His closely cropped hair and crisp shirt and tie indicated that he took care of his appearance. He sat straight in his chair, perhaps a habit from military days. In the initial phone call to Allworth Financial Jeannie had said her father was eighty-two years old, but he looked younger. Only his slightly rheumy brown eyes and oc-casional hand tremors indicated he was an octogenarian.

"But, Dad, I don't want you to just 'do all right.' I want you to be safe and around people who can love you and take care of you," Jeannie interjected.

"I can take care of myself! I don't need anyone else taking care of me," he said irritably.

"Ed, I can see that you enjoy your independence, just as I see that Jeannie wants to ensure your welfare and future happiness," Nicole broke in. "Could you tell me more about your days right now—what you enjoy doing, what you'd like to do more of or less of?"

"I enjoy woodworking in my garage," Ed said. "I like to read. I like to visit with my grandchildren and great-grandchildren, at least for a little while. I like to cook when I'm in the mood. I don't go out much, except to church, but that's by choice."

"Everything Dad does, he does by himself," Jeannie interrupted. "Mom was the social one who kept them involved. Now, Dad can go days without even leaving the house, except to go into the garage to work on his projects."

Adam leaned forward. "If Dad fell or got sick, and it wasn't one of Naomi's days to clean or bring by groceries, he could really be in trouble. Jeannie worries about him all the time."

"Ed, you've lived in Urbana for a while now, correct?" Josh asked.

"Yes. As Jeannie said, I taught at the university down there for twenty years. The kids all grew up there, and when I retired, Mattie and I decided to stay. As the kids grew older, they went in separate directions." Ed said. "Jeannie's the closest one to home, here in Chicago. The others are in Boston, Washington, D.C., Denver, and San Diego."

"You have five children?" Nicole asked. Even with multiple children available to share the care of an older parent, the responsibility often fell to one person.

"Yes, four boys and Jeannie. She's the youngest."

"I'm the favorite," Jeannie said, smiling at her father.

"Harrumph. I don't have favorites," Ed protested, but he looked at her and gave a slow wink. "She is my only daughter. She's bossy, but she tries to take care of everybody."

Nicole nodded once again. She had worked with many clients who were concerned about their aging parents' health and finances. She knew families could be irreparably divided by the difficult decisions children sometimes had to make on behalf of a parent, particularly when the parent had not stated preferences or figured out a plan—from end-of-life issues to who received Mom's wedding band. It was a good thing Ed was beginning to at least think about this now. Even though it was difficult to reconcile, Nicole knew that when Ed ensured that his own wishes were known, it would make Jeannie's and his other children's lives much easier.

"Ed, Jeannie makes a good point when she says that even though you're completely independent now, a time may come when that might not be the case," Josh began delicately. "You might get sick or incapacitated, or there may be a time when you no longer feel comfortable driving or getting around on your own. It often makes sense to look ahead so that if that time comes, your family can abide by the plan you've already mapped out. What would happen, for example, if you were to need additional help, perhaps on a daily basis?"

Ed looked at his hands, intertwined on the table. He sat silently, looking perplexed. "I guess I don't know," he said at last.

Everyone in the room felt Ed's pain as he acknowledged the truth. Josh remembered other clients talking about the moment they had to take away their parents' car keys because they were no longer able to drive, or create a power of attorney to help a parent who was no longer capable of making sound decisions. The child becomes the parent, and neither party welcomes that role reversal.

"Dad," Jeannie touched Ed's wrist again in that familiar way. "I don't want to take away your independence. I want to help you extend it for as long as you can. I think that if you have more support, you won't have to worry about as much, and you can do more woodworking or more cooking or whatever you like."

"We've talked about this before," Adam murmured to Nicole. "And he knows it's the right thing, but he's reluctant to make a change."

"Ed, in an ideal world, what would you like your life to be like for the next five, ten, fifteen years?" Usually Nicole talked with people about a longer time frame than that, but at his age, it made more sense to focus on the near future.

"I'd like to spend more time with the family. I'd like to have enough money to be comfortable. I don't need that much. But I do realize I'm getting old." Ed looked at Jeannie. "Your mother got sick and passed so quickly. She had a bad heart attack, and then had a second one, a fatal one, while she was in the hospital," he explained to Nicole and Josh. "Those last few days, when her heart was failing, she knew. She knew. And she told me she was glad that she wasn't lingering with months or years of slow decline, failing treatments, and hospice care. She saw several of her friends go through that, and she didn't want it. She didn't want us to have to do that." He turned to Josh and Nicole. "I'm the same way. I don't want my family to be burdened with my care. They may not see it as a burden, but I do. So how can we plan for the next five, ten, or however many years I have left so they won't have this worry?"

Josh looked Ed straight in the eyes and nodded. "Let's start talking about that," he said.

With Ed's agreement, Jeannie and Adam had sent his financial documents in advance as Josh and Nicole requested during their initial phone call.

"Our whole process here is designed to be educational," explained Nicole in a confident and calming voice. "So the main goal for today is to make sure that when you leave, you have a better handle on your financial situation than you did when you got here. So before we know where you're going, let's take a look at where you are financially right now."

As they reviewed Ed's portfolio, Josh and Nicole could see that he was a conservative man. He owned his single-family home and two cars—he hadn't been able to bring himself to sell Mattie's beloved Toyota Camry—and some old family property in South Carolina. He had income from his pension from the university, his Social Security, and dividends from some long-held investments in several blue chip companies. Within an hour, Nicole and Josh were able to explain the situation so that Ed's financial picture seemed clear to all involved.

A million dollars! Dad has more money than I knew, Jeannie thought, thanks to him and Mattie being frugal and living well within their means throughout life. But healthcare and assisted living costs were so expensive, she still wondered if it would be enough.

Mindful of the older man's energy level, Josh suggested a short break. On the way down the hall from the restroom, Ed pulled Josh aside. "Jeannie tells me I'm starting to repeat myself. Starting to forget things. Just little things, but still. I went to my doctor, and he said that it's to be expected with age, but he put me on some medicine just the same." Ed shook his head ruefully. "You know, they still can't diagnose Alzheimer's until after you're dead and they do an autopsy? I'm not saying I have that or dementia or anything more than trying to remember too many things at the age of eighty-two. I know I said I want to be independent—and I do. I don't want to burden Jeannie or one of my other kids with being my caretaker. I'm willing to consider other options. I just wanted you to know that." Having said his piece, Ed nodded firmly and walked back to the conference room.

It seemed to Josh that the father wanted to protect the child, and the child wanted to protect the father. As he followed Ed back into the room, his mind teemed with ideas for how to work toward accomplishing both goals.

"We have two questions to answer," Josh began once everyone reconvened. "How to create the lifestyle that Ed would like and that provides support, and how to ensure that his assets last as long as he needs them to so his children don't have either a financial or a caretaking burden.

"Ed is interested in considering other living arrangements that allow him to be as independent as possible, but also give increasing levels of support as his needs may change," Josh summarized. "Have you looked at any senior living communities yet?"

"No," Jeannie said, "at least not together. Adam and I have done some research, though, and we know that some of them are what they call continuing care retirement communities. Dad, you can move in there, into your own apartment or cottage, and if you need memory care or even skilled nursing, you can stay in the same community. Their websites talk about all of the onsite and offsite activities, events, and food. It makes me want to move in!"

"But they're expensive, and we aren't sure it is affordable, long term," Adam said.

"That's exactly what we can work out," Josh said. "We can look at some scenarios based on different options that will let you know what is affordable."

"I talked with Adam and my brothers about this, and we can each contribute to make sure Dad has what he needs." Jeannie said.

"Now, wait just a minute," Ed began.

"Dad, we want to help. You and Mom always helped us, and we want to do the same for you," Jeannie said.

"Let's take a look at those scenarios before we see if that's even necessary," Nicole said, just as Ed was about to speak. Jeannie and Ed obviously shared that same streak of independence, but Nicole was glad to see that father and daughter both wanted the best for the other. Some adult children only wonder how they can protect their own assets, regardless of an elderly parent's needs.

"As we look at these scenarios, there's another issue to address," Josh said. "Right now, Ed is able to make his own financial and health decisions. But what happens if that changes?" Josh felt a pang of regret that Ed's memory was slipping. He imagined Ed in his younger days, with that quiet authority and soldier's bearing. "We recommend talking with an elder law attorney to discuss drafting a trust."

"I'm sorry—what's a trust?" Jeannie said.

"With the proper asset protection trust, Ed would gift his money to you and your brothers now, so everything is out of his name except Social Security. There is a little more that goes into it, of course, but the attorneys will explain all that," Nicole explained. "It can reduce his taxes and, should the money run out, it will make it easier for him to qualify for Medicaid. But this trust is set up with the assumption that you and your siblings will manage all of Ed's expenses and not spend it otherwise. Ed, this type of planning should only be considered if you feel that the trustees, your children, will represent your interests if you're not able to."

"You mean you think they might run off to Vegas with my money?" Ed said with unexpected humor.

Nicole chuckled. "Hopefully not! But money can cause people to make bad decisions. The elder law attorney will want to make sure that you're making this decision of your own free will and that your kids will be able to work together to carry out your wishes and perhaps eventually make the best decisions for you."

"You have five children. If you establish a trust, you'll have to decide if you want one to be the trustee or if you want all of them to have equal say. Both choices can present some challenges, so give that some significant thought," Josh added. "It's a hard question, but if any of them are in a situation that could impair their judgment, they may not be the best person to be in charge of your money."

"What do you mean?" Adam asked.

"If any have financial difficulties, substance abuse or gambling problems, or mental illness that might make them tempted to use the money differently than it was intended, it's important to think about that and address it," Nicole explained. "Some parents don't want to hurt one child's feelings by not naming him or her as a trustee or decision maker, but that just makes it difficult for the rest of the kids. We've heard horror stories of older parents needing additional care but not having the finances available because their adult child blew through their funds. Those parents typically knew a particular child may not have been dependable but wanted to include him or her as a trustee anyway."

"I hear what you're saying, but Mattie and I have been fortunate. We have good kids," Ed said. "They dropped everything when Mattie got sick and came to see her. That meant everything to her. This one," he nodded to Jeannie, "keeps up with everybody. 'Have you heard from your brother?' she'll text one of them. 'You should call him.' And they do. She nags them, but they look forward to it."

Jeannie nodded. "We'd never do anything to hurt Dad."

"That's good to hear," Josh said. "Now that we know what Ed has to work with financially, we can estimate the maximum lifestyle his current assets and income can support. The next step is to find out how much he may realistically need. That will come once he's decided on living arrangements. We can estimate what he needs for living at home in Urbana, but we'll need to get financials from any senior living communities that he's considering to see what is needed for that."

"The other piece of the puzzle is developing the proper estate planning strategy. If that is the direction that you'd like to go in, we can recommend an elder law attorney and accompany you to the appointment to confirm whether a trust is appropriate," Nicole said.

It was a lot to take in. Although Ed had wanted to come to this meeting because he knew it was important, all the talk was about changing every aspect of his life. Leave his home. Move, perhaps, to another city. Give up his money. Sure, he trusted his children, but it was still hard—asking a man to turn over everything he had worked for his entire life. Even if that money was supposed to be used for him, the idea of not having anything left him feeling shaken.

"Why don't we go home and take some time to think about all we've discussed?" Jeannie suggested, looking closely at her dad.

"That sounds like a good idea," Josh agreed. "Call me in a few days . . . or whenever you are ready."

◎ ◎ ◎ When Jeannie called Josh later that week, she told him that her father had thought things through and, after talking with her brothers, did want to meet with the elder care attorney. He had also agreed to visit several continuing care retirement communities in the area.

"I think that's a great start, Jeannie," Josh said.

"We really appreciate your candor and guidance. You can help arrange a meeting with an elder law attorney, right?" Jeannie said.

"Absolutely. Elder law is highly specialized, and we have a relationship with one of the top firms in the country. The entire staff is very caring and knowledgeable. I think you'll like them."

Josh knew people felt more comfortable when all of their needs could be met in one spot. For that reason, Allworth Financial offered in-house services (e.g., accountants, estate planning, and divorce attorneys) to make it easier and more comfortable for clients. It was also easier to coordinate the entire process when he and Nicole were familiar with everyone involved, so they made sure to build good relationships with outside resources that shared the philosophy of practicing with the client's best interest in mind.

The next week, Josh and Nicole met with Jeannie and Ed at the elder law attorney's office. Melinda Commodore was a tall, lanky, former col-lege basketball player who had discovered a passion for law and for help-ing older adults secure their financial future. Raised by her grandparents, Melinda was just a teenager when her grandfather begrudgingly placed her grandmother in a nursing home. Her grandfather hadn't wanted to, but with his own frail health, he didn't have the strength to lift his wife in and out of bed. Melinda's grandmother had developed dementia, and while she and her grandfather could initially handle keeping her from leaving the apartment in her nightgown or accidentally leaving the burner on, she eventually needed more assistance with daily maintenance. Feed-ing her was easy, but bathing her, taking her to the toilet, and turning her to prevent bedsores became more than the two could handle. With little savings, the nursing home was the best Melinda's grandfather could find, but it still wasn't very comforting. The hallways were dark and a little scary to Melinda as a teenager. The nurses were often abrupt. Although she never saw anyone mistreat a patient, she sometimes heard families of other patients complain about the care.

Six months after Melinda's grandmother moved into the nursing home, she died. Her grandfather held on for another three years, deter-mined to last until Melinda turned eighteen. He died that year in March of pneumonia, refusing to go to the hospital. Melinda knew that regardless of their finances, she wanted people to have more options than her grandparents had, and she focused on using laws that would help do that.

After introductions were made and everyone was seated in Melinda's office, she began. "Before we actually get into the meeting, I'd like to speak with Ed alone," she said. Nicole had explained beforehand that Melinda would want to make sure Ed was of sound mind and not being pressured into this decision. Jeannie, Nicole, and Josh stepped out of the office and into the hallway.

"We visited three retirement communities this week," Jeannie told Nicole. "Dad really liked one of them, so when we come for our follow-up with you, we'd like to see how to make this work."

"Absolutely. We'll get that on the calendar as soon as we're done here," Nicole said.

After a few minutes, Melinda motioned for Jeannie, Nicole, and Josh to return to the office and waited for them to settle into their seats.

"Okay, let's talk about how we'll set up this trust," Melinda said, mak-ing eye contact with Ed. She always tried to include the parent in the conversation. Too many people assumed the elderly were completely incompetent, but Melinda made a point of treating those clients with the utmost respect. "I'll go into the details in a minute, but just so you have an overview, we'll outline the trust and have the attorney draft it. After you've had a chance to review it, we'll meet again and sign it. At that time, any child or children who will be trustees will need to be present to sign the paperwork as well. Then, you can take the trust to Josh and Nicole to ensure we can fund it properly."

"So how long is this process?" Jeannie asked.
"It's normally a three- to four-week process to get the trust drafted and implemented. After that point, Ed, if you've found an assisted living community that you like, you can make plans to move in," Melinda said.

❍ ❍ ❍   In their follow-up meeting at Allworth Financial two weeks later, Jeannie showed Nicole a brochure of the retirement community Ed had selected.

"This is the one he likes. It has lots of activities every day, including cooking classes," Jeannie said.

"And it has apartments with attached garages, so I can set up my workbench," Ed added. "And no outside maintenance. No shoveling snow, even in Chicago." He chuckled. "How about that?"

Nicole looked at Ed, wondering about the change in his mood. He was more relaxed than he had been at their earlier meeting, and he seemed less defensive. He sounded enthusiastic—guardedly, perhaps—but with an eager tone in his voice.

"The question is, can we make this happen? We have the trust drawn up now, but does Dad have enough to fund it?" Jeannie asked, handing Nicole and Josh the prospective package Ed had received from the community. "We know the current costs, but if Dad needs more care, his costs will increase. How can we make sure he has enough?"

Josh and Nicole looked through the package, and then Nicole opened up a folder that had a simple spreadsheet on one page, pointing to numbers as she talked. "Right now, this community will cost you $5,000 a month. Those costs will obviously increase as you need more care. We went through the financial information you gave us. Ed, with your current assets and income, and assuming the sale of your house, it certainly appears as if you could afford to live in a place like this community for the next ten years. To add to the good news, you may also be eligible to receive additional income in the future, based on your status as a veteran."

"I was in the Army for six years, served during the Korean War," Ed said proudly.

"We appreciate your service," Josh said sincerely.

"It was the right thing to do," Ed said.

"It was still a sacrifice, and it shouldn't go unnoticed," Josh responded. It wasn't just a rote phrase. Like Josh, most of his friends had chosen college or jobs after high school, not the military. The concept of putting your life at risk, to go where you were ordered to go, to train to defend your country . . . it was not to be glossed over or taken for granted.

"You were saying about the veteran's benefits?" Jeannie prompted.

"Yes," Nicole continued. "This will only apply when you need assistance with two or more of your daily living activities. At that point, we can apply for Veteran's Aid and Attendance benefits, which will help offset some of your expenses and allow your money to last longer or pass remaining assets on to the kids."

"I'm confused," Jeannie said. "What kind of benefits can he get in assisted living?"

"It's called Aid and Attendance benefit," Josh said. "A lot of people are unaware of it, but it helps with long-term care. Most senior living communities charge more when a resident needs a higher level of individual care, such as with bathing or feeding. The Aid and Attendance benefit provides additional funds to help pay for that extra care," he explained. "We'll keep that in mind for the future, if needed. Once we set up the trust, it will also transfer your investments so Jeannie and the boys will able to make payments on your behalf. We can help establish a budget to cover current and anticipated needs. And, in a worst-case scenario, if all of your funds are exhausted, you can remain in this community by applying for Medicaid."

"So once Dad moves in, he won't have to move out, not unless he wants to," Jeannie confirmed.

"That's right," Josh said. "He'll have the security and safety you want, and the activity and independence he wants."

Ed leaned back in his seat. He sometimes did that, letting the conversations swirl around him. He still tuned into the important comments, but he could let his thoughts drift to Mattie. "Don't be a jackass, Ed," she'd tell him, in her own tough but kind way, if she were here. A Navy brat herself, she never failed to surprise him with her somewhat salty language. This was the right thing to do. The thought of packing up his house, his entire world, momentarily overwhelmed him, and he closed his eyes, rubbing his forehead. "It's just stuff, Ed," Mattie would say. "Don't let your stuff keep you from living your life!"

Jeannie had called him out before, saying he never did anything. She was right. He hadn't been living his life. Truth be told, he had been going through the motions, all while he had been grieving his wife. Maybe a complete shakeup was what he needed to give himself permission to enjoy however much time he had left. Ed opened his eyes and sighed, blowing away emotion. Then, placing his palms on the table, he leaned into the conversation.

"So, how do we get this going?" he asked.

Josh smiled, looking forward to helping Ed and his family create his new future.

ELDER CARE: ADVICE FROM JOSH AND NICOLE

With all of our clients, our first step is to understand their complete financial picture. The next step is to ensure that the clients understand that same picture. The formula is often the same, but with each person, there are usually specific areas where we can make significant differences.

It's not easy when an adult child begins to take on more responsibility for an older parent. There may be resentment and denial on both ends, but ultimately, the goal is—or at least, should be—to ensure that the parent is in a safe, comfortable, stimulating environment and that the parent's funds can sustain that lifestyle for as long as necessary. Making sure everyone involved in the parent's financial decisions is on the same page is key. Consulting with a reputable elder law attorney is instrumental in creating a plan that guides and protects both the parent and the adult child.

Ed and his family were unaware of some of the benefits he was entitled to through his military service. Those additional funds could be useful as his care needs increase. For information on the VA Aid and Attendance benefit, contact the U.S. Department of Veteran's Affairs (*http://benefits. va.gov/pension/aid_attendance_housebound.asp*).

Another important piece in Ed's situation was informing him how Medicaid is administered. Multiple rules guide how much money a person can have and still qualify for Medicaid. In addition, Medicaid looks at how the person's finances have been distributed in previous years to ensure the person is truly eligible. It's critical to create a plan that balances current and future needs to make sure funds are available as long as needed. For more information on Medicaid and to determine your local resource, check the national Medicaid website, *www.medicaid.gov*.

CONVERSATIONS TO HAVE WITH FAMILY

1. In the event of an illness, does your family know how you would like to be cared for? Do they know what assets you have and where they are held?

2. Do you understand the different levels of care and the associated costs of care for your particular family member in your geographic area?

3. Was the affected person or their spouse actively engaged in the

military at any point during their life? If so, do you have copies of the discharge papers?

4. Research elder care attorneys in your area.

5. Is there "asset preservation estate planning" in your state?

CHAPTER 9

FINDING HERSELF
CLIENT STORY: DOROTHY GREEN

"THE GREATEST THING IN THE WORLD
IS TO KNOW HOW TO BELONG TO ONESELF."
Michel de Montaigne, French Renaissance Writer

Dorothy Green looked at the letter in front of her in disbelief. Sixty thousand dollars? How was it possible to owe that much in taxes? Her hand shook as she stood in the shady hallway of her Hyde Park townhome. Maybe she'd misread it, she reassured herself as she walked to the kitchen, forgetting the remaining mail she'd left on the table by the entryway. She'd get her glasses and look again.

But even sitting under the bright light that hung over the oak kitchen table, with her reading glasses perched on the end of her nose, the numbers were the same. Taxes owed for fourth quarter, 2006. It must be a mistake, one that could be settled with a phone call, she hoped. Once again, as had been happening with increasing frequency, Dorothy felt her age of seventy-five. She prided herself on not being an old crotchety widow. She walked regularly, keeping trim. She went to the beauty salon every two weeks to ensure her salt and pepper pixie kept enough of its pepper. She read the newspaper every day to stay up to date on what was going on in the world. She had lunch with friends, attended social events, and talked with her children to stay connected. She volunteered for a charity and attended events at the nearby University of Chicago to keep her mind and emotions stimulated. Yet, since Henry's death two years ago, Dorothy had felt fragile. In the previous six months, she had become more adept at hiding that vulnerability, purposefully walking briskly into rooms, giving bright smiles and inquiring about the days of others. But then, something would throw her. She'd be faced with something like this financial statement or another financial issue or even a home or auto repair decision, and in those moments, Dorothy admitted to herself that she felt utterly lost.

"Damn you, Henry," she allowed herself to whisper sadly. If only she'd had more warning—more time to prepare. But who could have predicted that Henry would have a fatal aneurysm as he trudged outside to pick up his morning copy of the *Chicago Tribune* from their walkway? Henry had taken care of all of the financial decisions. As the man of the house and a savvy business owner, it made sense. Nowadays, plenty of women handle the finances for the family, but things were different when Dorothy and Henry married in 1951. Marriages were very traditional, and while Henry had a career, Dorothy focused on the family. Dorothy was comfortable in that role even though she was one of the few women of her age who had advanced to earn a college degree. Henry was a good husband and had always taken care of her and their three children, Henry Jr., Catherine, and John. Having grown up during the Depression, Henry and Dorothy had always been frugal with their money. Dorothy's children had never understood why she reused aluminum foil or holiday wrapping paper, carefully refolding it and putting it away.

"Mom, you can buy more!" they said, but they had never experienced the uncertainty of knowing if their father would be working the next day or if they could get foods that were in short supply. Maybe she and Henry should have explained their reasoning to the kids in more detail, but pre-World War II had been a painful era that neither of them wanted to revisit. They preferred not to discuss money and were just happy that they could provide for their kids—maybe not everything the children wanted, but certainly a nice home, healthy food, warm clothes, interesting books, and a good education. They never went without what they needed, and Dorothy and Henry didn't mind waiting for what they wanted.

As Dorothy looked at the notice in her hand, she briefly thought about calling one of her children for help but quickly dismissed the idea. She loved her children, but she was not blind to their weaknesses, and finances were one of them. Even as adults, and Catherine with children of her own, they tended to let money slip through their fingers, accumulating credit card debt that made a Depression-era person shudder. No, Dorothy needed to talk to someone who understood money management. Her accountant, James Richards, had taken care of her taxes for twenty years, well before Henry died. James called Dorothy occasionally to ask her a question or request clarification, but Dorothy didn't really have an answer or an opinion. "Just do what you think is best. Do what Henry would do," she told him. James had called her a day earlier, leaving a voice message asking if she had received the tax bill and if she had any questions. That sent Dorothy scrambling to look through the day's mail to find the bill. She always paid the water and electric bill promptly, but they were never as atrociously expensive as the one she held in her hand.

What would Henry do now? Since Henry's death, she had hidden her head in the sand like the proverbial ostrich, but now there was no one to handle this outrageous bill but her, and it had to be handled. Sighing, she pushed up from the table and walked over to the counter, reaching for the telephone and her address book next to it. Her children kept telling her she should get a cell phone, and even some of her friends had one, but everyone who needed to reach her could, and if she missed a call, she had her reliable answering machine right next to the phone. Dorothy looked up the number to James' office and dialed.

"Dorothy," James' melodious voice was soothing as he greeted her. "It's great to hear from you."

"Hello, James," Dorothy said, uncharacteristically abrupt. "I just got this bill that makes no sense to me. It says I owe over sixty thousand dollars in taxes. What does that mean? How did that happen?"

James swallowed a sigh. "Dorothy," he began gently. "Remember we talked about this a few weeks ago? I called as soon as I realized the implications of that bill. You said you wanted to wait to talk until you'd had a chance to see it."

Dorothy shook her head impatiently. She hadn't forgotten, but she also hadn't wanted to remember. "Well, I'm looking at it now. So tell me, what happened?"

"I'm not sure, Dorothy, but I'll find out. It may be a result of your investments. Have you made any financial changes lately?" James asked.

Dorothy blushed. She had no idea. Henry had established some investment accounts with another financial institution years ago, and since his death, she hadn't even bothered to open the monthly statements.

"Not that I'm aware of," she said carefully.

"Here's what I'll do," James said. "Let me talk with your advisor. I'll get the scoop and call you back, okay?"

"Yes. Thank you so much, James," Dorothy said. She hung up the phone. If the tax bill was correct, how would she pay it? The townhouse was paid for, as was her car, and she knew Henry had set up an account so she could live comfortably within her means, but how much of that savings would be left once the tax bill was paid? She didn't know.

It didn't help matters when James called her later that afternoon and explained that her broker had inadvertently moved money from her IRA account into her trust account last year, which created this huge tax bill.

"So there's nothing I can do?" Dorothy said faintly.

"Not about the tax bill, I'm afraid," James said. "You can easily liquidate some of your holdings to cover it."

"Oh, dear, well, can you take care of that?" Dorothy asked, hating the tremulousness in her voice. She was doing it again. Sticking her head back in the sand.

Asking someone else to take care of her life. "Suck it up, Grandma," her twenty-year-old granddaughter, Kiki, often advised her. Kiki, Catherine's daughter, often had more wisdom and moxie than her mother. *All right. I'm sucking it up*, Dorothy thought.

"James," she amended, "I am not happy at all with the way the company handled this. I may not have been paying attention, but I pay them so I don't have to!"

Henry had trusted this company, but she knew he would be outraged about this, too. She may not venture into the financial world too often, but her instincts about the world were often spot on, and her gut was telling her to look for a company she could trust.

"I understand how you feel," James agreed. "Your current investment company is well known, but they're so large, they may not be able to give you the personal attention you need. I mentioned a place to you a few years ago called Allworth Financial Did you ever get in touch with them?"

"I believe I may have talked to someone over there before, but frankly, I had so much going on after Henry died, I'm afraid I never contacted them again," Dorothy admitted.

"You might want to give them another look. They're located in the suburbs near my office, and they pay attention to our clients and encourage an educational and conservative long-term approach," James said. "Allworth Financial is run by Josh Kadish. I think you'll like him, and he personally handles all of my finances."

Josh Kadish. The name sounded vaguely familiar. Yes. As Dorothy thought back, she remembered calling Josh on James' recommendation two years ago. Josh was friendly when Dorothy called, but as soon as they began talking, Dorothy froze. In those dark months after Henry died, it was impossible to even contemplate making any changes, financial or otherwise. "I'm just not ready," she had explained to Josh back then.

"Of course," Josh said. "That is absolutely understandable. Please just remember that if you ever want to talk things through—whether you want to make changes or not—I'm here. Take as long as you need."

Dorothy had appreciated that Josh didn't try to sell anything to her or push her into making changes. Instead, he was willing to let her go at her own pace. At that time, of course, she wasn't going at any pace at all. But now, maybe she was ready for baby steps.

"That sounds good," Dorothy told James as she continued clutching the tax bill. "I'll call him."

⊘ ⊘ ⊘ A week later, Dorothy and Josh sat down at a family-owned deli in Chicago. After the waiter took her order, Dorothy appraised Josh. Even though it had been two years since they talked, he still remembered her. When she suggested a meeting, he offered to meet her midway between his office and her home, so she suggested one of her favorite restaurants. He was young, Dorothy thought. But at seventy-five, she now thought even new senior citizens looked young. He was maybe late thirties, early forties, with a wedding ring. That was good. She liked it when men proudly wore a symbol of their marriage. Dorothy rubbed her own wedding band. Some friends had suggested it was time to take it off, but she couldn't understand why. She wasn't going to remarry, and she rather liked having the memories of Henry as close as her finger.

"I received news of a rather astronomical tax bill last week," she said as the waiter left. "My accountant found out that it was a slip on behalf of my current financial advisors. Naturally, I'm concerned about them handling my savings in the future, and I'm also worried about how this debt will affect my lifestyle going forward."

Josh nodded, patiently listening.

"If you ask me about my finances, I'm afraid I won't be much help. My husband handled that, and frankly, I don't know much about it," Dorothy added.

"I can certainly understand your situation," Josh said. "We've worked with many clients who realized after a mistake or mishandling that they were not as familiar with their finances as they would like to be. They've felt helpless. No one wants to feel like that. That's why I believe that the first step is to help you understand exactly what your financial picture looks like. When you're educated in your finances, you're no longer at anyone's mercy."

"That may be true, but I really have no clue about anything. I know Henry has some stocks, but I don't know what they are. I use a checking account that James deposits money into from my savings every month, but that's the depth of my knowledge," Dorothy said.

"Do you have bank or financial statements?" he asked.

"This is going to sound very bad, but I have several shoe boxes in my guest closet. When the mail comes and it's one of those, I just put it in the shoe box and push the box to the back of my closet floor," Dorothy confessed, expecting Josh to lecture her on the importance of responsibility.

"That's great. We have a start," Josh assured her.

"But it's a shoebox filled with unopened envelopes."

"Dorothy," Josh said gently, "it's not a monster. Just some folded up papers. We can help you go through them one by one, at your pace. Wouldn't you feel better if you weren't afraid of those envelopes? Wouldn't you like to know how much you have instead of being afraid you don't have enough? Can you imagine how that could change your outlook?"

Tears began to escape from Dorothy's light brown eyes. With the exception of her best friend, Micki, no one else had talked with her so sincerely about *her* best interests. Sure, she had received advice, solicited and otherwise, but it was always tinged with a sense of what the advisor would gain. Josh seemed to be concerned about Dorothy's needs, not about a product she should buy.

"I suppose you're right," Dorothy agreed. *Suck it up*, she reminded herself. "How do we even start?"

"We get the monsters out of the closet," Josh said with a grin. "I'm going to ask you to gather up all of those envelopes—statements you have from your bank or any financial institution. We'll start from scratch and figure everything out together. With your permission, I can also talk through things with James, as he certainly knows the most about your finances after twenty years of helping Henry."

That sounded possible, Dorothy thought. Henry used to tease her because she always seemed to get involved in projects, whether they were at school or in the neighborhood when the children were young, or with volunteer organizations later. Dorothy might come home from a meeting grousing about the amount of work to be done, but her eyes would be sparkling from the challenge. As she contemplated the work ahead, she felt a little anxious, but the thought of being in control of her money also gave her just a little bit of excitement.

◐ ◐ ◐ A month later, Dorothy met again with Josh, this time in his office downtown. She had organized her piles of shoebox envelopes into categories: bank, investments, insurance, and medical. She'd secured each pile with a rubber band, stuffed them all into a large manila envelope, and mailed them to Josh's office. He called her when he received them and said he would go through the statements and put them in a format that would be easier to review. Today, Josh would help her go through that information.

After some small talk, Dorothy looked expectantly at Josh. "Should we get started?"

"Sure," Josh reached for a folder from the credenza behind his big black leather chair. He took out a binder filled with about two inches of paper in it. Dorothy saw her name typed at the top of the first one.

"I put your financial picture together and consolidated it into an easy to understand format for you. Let's start by looking at this page. It's your consolidated net worth statement that shows you on one page everything you have," Josh said.

Dorothy put on her reading glasses.

"Here are the investments you have, from the savings and checking to the investment accounts at your current broker to your townhouse in Hyde Park. We add up everything you have and subtract out what you owe and that gives us your total net worth." Josh used his pen to point to each number, looking up at Dorothy to ensure she was following along.

Dorothy frowned as she looked at the total. "This is what again?"

"This is how much money you have, Dorothy. You have roughly five million dollars."

Dorothy was stunned. "That can't be."

"I checked and double checked and confirmed all of this with your accountant," Josh said. "With a tax bill so high, I anticipated that you might have a significant portfolio."

"So I can pay my tax bill?" Dorothy asked.

"Yes, you can pay your tax bill, and probably not even notice the money is missing. But I wouldn't recommend you do that on a regular basis," Josh said with a light-hearted grin. "The point is, Dorothy, that you have a very healthy portfolio. You can likely do anything you want." Josh smiled and waited for that information to sink in.

"I don't know what I want to do," Dorothy said.

"That's okay. As we go through this process, you may start figuring it out."

"Go through the process?" Dorothy asked. "We're not done?"

"I hope not!" Josh said. "You now know what your assets are. But *where* are they? How are they invested, and is that what's appropriate for you? Some of your investments are fairly risky, in my opinion. But you should consider what you'd like. And eventually we get to the long-term planning. What do you want to do next? Do you want to stay in your townhouse or move? What needs might you have as you get older that you'll want to anticipate now? What—"

"I understand!" Dorothy interrupted with a little laugh. "I see that there's more to learn. All right, young man. Let's get this lesson started."

Josh met with Dorothy every few months over the next seven years, at first helping her understand different aspects of her portfolio and eventually helping her develop a financial plan. Initially, she primarily listened, occasionally asking questions. Then, she began to start the meetings with questions about how events in the financial world were affecting her holdings.

"You're right. There is too much risk in my investments," she said one day. "If the stock market is headed for a correction, some of these stocks I have will be adversely affected. What can we do to be a little more conservative?" Josh looked at her, as proud as any teacher could be of his pupil.

In one of their regular meetings in 2011, Dorothy was pleased to meet Nicole, who had joined the firm since Dorothy's last visit. *She's kind*, Dorothy assessed, as they talked. *And intelligent. Not the type to get caught with an unexpected tax bill,* Dorothy thought, still with a lingering sense of chagrin. Then she silently reminded herself that the tax bill fiasco was in the past—over and done.

"I'm thinking about moving," Dorothy announced at her meeting with Josh that day. She had lived in her townhouse for thirty years and was ready for a change. While she would never leave her beloved city, she conceded that Chicago winters were cold, windy, and sometimes danger-ously icy. Last winter, she spent two weeks inside after a snowstorm, not wanting to risk slipping. There were plenty of restaurants and stores in the neighborhood that delivered, but she didn't like giving up her inde-pendence—going out when she wanted to. "My friend Micki is planning on moving into a very nice retirement community on Lake Shore Drive. It's all located in a high rise. There are apartments, a gym, restaurants, and even some little shops. I'm considering joining her."

"That sounds exciting, but also like a big change," Nicole said.

"I know. The idea of going through our belongings, knowing I couldn't fit them all into a new place, is a bit overwhelming. So much of Henry's things I still haven't touched," Dorothy admitted.

"Could your children help you?" Nicole asked.

Dorothy hesitated. "Maybe. But they don't come in town very often, and when they do, I want to be able to just go out and enjoy my time with them. To be honest, I haven't told them that I'm planning on moving yet."

"Do you think they'll be upset about that?" Josh asked.

"Not so much that. Do you remember, Josh, when you sat down

and told me what my net worth was, and how shocked I was? Well, my children have no idea what my financial situation is, and I've preferred to keep it that way. I've continued to live fairly modestly, but this retirement community is definitely more luxurious than what I'm used to. They'll begin to ask questions like how much money I have, and inevitably, when can they get some?"

"So you are concerned that they'll pressure you to give them money?" With her particular interest in helping older adults manage their finances, Nicole's antenna went up when it sounded like Dorothy's adult children might try to unduly influence their elderly mother's financial decisions.

"I think that my children have not done a very good job of managing the money they have earned, and I am concerned they will look at this as a second, third, or fourth chance, when they never learned the lesson the first time," Dorothy admitted.

"We worked with you on your trust a few years ago," Josh said. "You'll be leaving the bulk of your estate to your children. Would it make sense to start talking with them about this now? Help them prepare?"

"Perhaps it would. But I'm just not ready to do that at this time. I'm making enough changes for an old lady as it is." Dorothy chuckled lightly, but her voice was firm. "Right now, let's talk about what this potential move would look like, financially."

Josh and Nicole outlined the money Dorothy could get from the sale of her townhouse. Then they looked at the brochure Dorothy brought from the retirement community that described several financial options for entering the community, and they helped her figure out how they could affect her.

Even after the financing was figured out, Dorothy wasn't quite ready to move. It took a year, one more Chicago winter, before she signed the paperwork for her new home, with Micki beaming beside her.

A few months after she moved in, Dorothy invited Josh to see her new place.

"It's beautiful," Josh said as he took in the skyline view from Dorothy's living room. Dorothy would never spend money on a decorator, but she had done a nice job of making her new apartment her home, with walls covered in old family photos interspersed with beautiful, hand-signed original art—probably worth thousands of dollars unbeknownst to Dorothy, but priceless to her for the memories of her past. Neutral colors with some subtle splashes of pinks and peach thrown in, and this dwelling declared itself as Dorothy's feminine domain.

"Thank you," Dorothy said as she brought two glasses of ice water from the kitchen. "I'm really enjoying it. People are always around if I want to go into the common areas, but I have my privacy when I want. And I have so many activities I can do! I just don't have enough time to do them all!"

"I'm so glad this has worked well for you," Josh said as he sat on the cream-colored sofa. "How did your children react when you told them about the move?"

"They were surprised, but they actually handled it better than I thought. Catherine and John even flew in to help me pack and move. I know they have questions, but no one wants to be the first to ask how I can afford to live here. Dorothy's eyes twinkled in amusement.

"So have you given any more thought to talking with them about finances?" Josh didn't want to nag, but part of his job was to make sure he helped his clients be prepared. As part of Dorothy's family, her children were also his clients, and he wanted to help them make good choices, regardless of Dorothy's money. He could help them figure out their own finances, independent of hers, and help them create a budget and a plan.

"All in good time, Josh," Dorothy said, taking a sip from her glass of Lake Michigan's finest.

Josh was silent as they sat, taking in the view. He knew he could only nudge his client a little at a time, even if it was for her own good. She had already come so far, from stuffing all of her financial statements in a shoebox to making informed, thoughtful financial decisions. She just needed to do it at her pace. He would be patient.

Dorothy looked around her home with satisfaction. "For the first time," she continued softly, "I'm not Henry's wife. I'm not someone's mother. I'm me. I'm Dorothy."

AFTER THE LOSS OF A SPOUSE: ADVICE FROM JOSH AND NICOLE

When a loved one dies, it can be extremely overwhelming, particularly if it was the person who primarily handled the finances. Although it is tempting to stick all financial information into a shoebox, ultimately, not knowing what's coming up can add more stress. While big financial decisions should be postponed until you feel more settled, some decisions should be made quickly, such as understanding expenses and income.

The next section, "Tips for Handling Finances after the Loss of a Loved One," provides a general list of what aspects to handle first.

Although Dorothy was intimidated about learning the details of her finances and was a little embarrassed that she didn't already know them, she felt a strong sense of empowerment once she had the education and confidence to make decisions. Finding an advisor who is focused on educating, and not just directing, is key to helping you become your own best advisor. Be sure to ask questions and follow your gut feeling about those with whom you work.

TIPS FOR HANDLING FINANCES AFTER THE LOSS OF A LOVED ONE

1. **Assess your cash flow.** While you should postpone big financial decisions, you should take stock quickly of your expenses and income. Make a list of your income sources: Social Security, pension payments, dividends, interest, job earnings, and IRA distributions.

    Write down your fixed expenses, such as groceries, mortgage payments, utilities, and insurance. Check your deceased spouse's check register, too. Make a separate list for your discretionary costs, such as gifts and travel.

    As you assess your cash flow, remember that some income payments may decline. For instance, if your husband was receiving a Social Security benefit and you were getting a 50% spousal benefit, the spousal benefit will disappear. But some expenses will end as well, such as your spouse's Medicare premiums.

    If you are short on cash, start chipping away on the discretionary spending.

    Build a reserve for one to two years of expenses in a liquid account, such as a bank money-market account.

2. **Collect life insurance benefits.** If you can't find the life insurance policy and you don't have an agent, go through checkbook registers and canceled checks to see if there were any checks written to an

insurance company. For a fee, the MIB Solutions' Policy Locator Service (*www.policylocator.com*) might help you find the application. Your spouse also may have had a group policy through an employer or former employer or professional or fraternal organizations.

When you file a claim, you may have choices regarding how you will receive the money. Read the fine print carefully. In some cases, an insurance company will place your funds into its own money-market funds and send you a checkbook. Turn down this option, and then place the money in a federally insured bank account or a money-market fund. If you're instead considering guaranteed monthly payments for life, seek the advice of your lawyer or financial advisor.

3. **Prepare the estate.** Until you meet with your estate lawyer, hold off on placing your spouse's assets in your own name. If you touch assets in your spouse's name, you'll lose any opportunity to "disclaim" the property—that is, allowing those assets to go directly to your children or other heirs. If you forgo these assets, they will not count against your federal or state estate-tax exemption when you die.

   You have nine months from the date of your spouse's death to file a federal estate-tax return. Some states have earlier deadlines for filing returns for state estate and inheritance taxes.

   Save all receipts related to the estate, especially if the estate's value is close to or exceeds the estate-tax exemption.

   Assuming you had named your spouse to make financial and healthcare decisions on your behalf in the event you became incapacitated, you will need to designate a new agent for your financial power of attorney, healthcare power of attorney, and healthcare directive.

4. **Check with the employer.** If your spouse was employed at the time of death, call the benefits administrator to ask about benefits due to you. Besides life insurance, these can include unpaid salary and bonuses, accrued vacation and sick pay, leftover funds in a medical flexible spending account, and stock options.

   You'll also need to check on pension benefits. Assuming your spouse was retired and you were both receiving monthly pension benefits in the form of a joint and survivor annuity, notify the plan administrator immediately. Depending on the type of annuity you chose, you could be due part or all of what both of you were receiving before your spouse died.

If you were receiving health coverage under your spouse's employer plan, you may be able to continue on the group plan for 36 months through COBRA coverage. (An employer with fewer than 20 employees is not required to provide COBRA coverage.) Ask the plan administrator if the company will continue picking up the employer's premium subsidy.

5. **Roll over an IRA.** If you are the only beneficiary of your spouse's IRA, you can roll the retirement plan into your own IRA tax free. (You must take other steps if you are one of several beneficiaries.)

6. **Claim a Social Security benefit.** A widow or widower is entitled to a survivor benefit that is equal to 100% of the deceased spouse's benefit, as long as the survivor waits until full retirement age to collect. You can collect a survivor benefit as early as 60, but your benefit will be permanently reduced a bit for each month you claim before your full retirement age. (It's reduced by 28.5% if you claim at 60.)

If you were collecting a spousal benefit, you can "step up" to a survivor benefit. At that point, the spousal benefit will disappear. If you are younger than full retirement age and decide to wait to claim the full survivor benefit, you will stop receiving the spousal benefit. If your husband dies before claiming a benefit, you will be eligible for a survivor benefit equal to the benefit he was entitled to at the time of his death.

We encourage you to contact your attorney or financial planner to help you through this financial transition.

CHAPTER 10

FOR THE FAMILY
CLIENT STORY: JOSEPH AND BELLE SILVA

"A YEAR FROM NOW YOU WILL WISH YOU
HAD STARTED TODAY."

Karen Lamb, Director, The Miracle You Learning Center

"I'm ready to retire," Joseph Silva announced to Josh and Nicole as soon as they were settled around the conference room table.

"He says that every time we meet, doesn't he?" His wife, Belle, smiled at Josh and Nicole as she nudged her husband's arm.

"He does," Josh agreed, smiling. "And it's been, what, about eight years?"

In that time, the couple had hardly changed. Joseph's company had contacted Allworth Financial to offer a retirement seminar for the company's mid- and upper-level executives aged fifty and over. Since he was fifty-five years old, Joseph attended. The moment Josh started talk-ing about aspects of retirement, Joseph realized that although he *wanted* to retire, he had made few preparations to make that happen.

"How much money do you need in order live the lifestyle you want?" Josh had asked. It sounded simple, but Joseph hadn't thought about it. What lifestyle *did* he want? He and Belle lived in a house in the suburbs of Chicago, but now that their only child, Michael, had left for college in Atlanta, the house seemed too big, too empty, for just the two of them. Even though Michael came home for breaks, Joseph could already tell that his independent son would never return to live at home perma-nently. Chicago winters were brutal—much different from the winters he experienced growing up after his parents emigrated from Colombia to Texas. Belle's family was mostly in Miami, and Joseph enjoyed them as if they were his own. He would love spending more time with them, outside the special occasion, birthday, holiday, or anniversary celebration.

With those initial thoughts in mind, Joseph had been eager to more seriously plan for retirement, and since Allworth Financial offered a discount to company employees who wanted to receive individual coun-seling sessions, Joseph made an appointment with Josh.

"I want to retire," Joseph said at the time. "I've been with this company for thirty-five years and frankly, I'm tired. I've seen more changes, more comings and goings, than I'd like, and I know it's just going to be more of the same." He looked up at Josh, challengingly. "What can you do for me?"

"I can certainly appreciate that you've dedicated yourself to your company," Josh began. He recognized Joseph's frustration but also knew the answers may not be the ones Joseph wanted to hear. "In the workshop, we talked about envisioning your future lifestyle, and that will play a big part in determining when you can retire. We can figure out how much money you have right now and how much you think you'll need to spend to maintain the lifestyle you've dreamed about. We can then project how things might play out financially over the next ten, twenty, and even thirty years down the road. When we complete that analysis, we'll have a much clearer picture of what might be a realistic goal for your retirement."

As Josh and the Silvas worked on creating a complete financial picture, Joseph realized it was not economically feasible to retire yet. Because they were still so young, he and Belle realistically needed to have money to last the next thirty to thirty-five years. They were still paying Michael's tuition, and their budgets would be stretched tight.

"I'm sorry, Jose," Belle said, using her nickname for him. "I know this isn't what you wanted to hear."

"It's a wakeup call, that's for sure," Joseph said. "I guess I just hoped we'd magically have enough money. I didn't actually think about the details and how strapped we would be for the rest of our lives if I did retire now."

"The good news is, now you do know—before you make a huge

life change," Josh reminded Joseph. "And you know what you need to do—how much to save each month in your 401(k) plan and elsewhere. You know the return you'll need and subsequently have an idea of how much risk you should be taking to accomplish your long-term goals and dreams." Josh paused while Joseph digested that information. "Now you can make decisions going forward with confidence, knowing you'll have the money needed to enjoy your concept of retirement."

Since that day, the Silvas continued to meet regularly with Josh and, later, with both Josh and Nicole to update their retirement analysis and review their progress to make sure they were on track. Sometimes Josh or Nicole would suggest a change to their savings or investment allocation to manage their overall risk and work toward reaching their goals.

Now, eight years later, Josh surveyed the couple. Joseph still looked robust as ever, perhaps with more silver streaking through his hair. Belle, as usual, was striking, with a newly cropped hairdo that framed her face well. *Sophia Loren*, Josh thought.

"I know I've said I wanted to retire before," Joseph said, "but this time I'm ready. My company has offered some of us dinosaurs a retirement package." He took out a manila envelope and pulled out a bound booklet, handing it to Nicole. "Take a look. It's for my entire group," he explained.

Nicole thumbed through the papers. "This looks like a generous package. I'd like to take a closer look at the numbers after we're finished talking here. Joseph, I know you've been saying all along that you are ready to retire, but this is still a voluntary package, so it's still your choice. Are you sure this is what you want?"

"That's a good point," Josh agreed. "We talked about sixty-two as being the earliest that you'd retire, with you having increasing options the longer you work. I don't want to push you to do something you don't want to, but I just want to ensure that you're thinking long term."

Joseph glanced at Belle, who looked down at her hands.

"I'm sure." He patted Belle's hands. "You know our grandson, Jay?"

Nicole nodded. Joseph often talked about his son, Michael; Michael's wife, Sofia; and their three-year-old son, Jay. The first meeting after Jay was born, Joseph said he wanted to start a college savings fund for his newborn grandchild. At every visit, Joseph proudly shared photos of the little boy.

"He's been sick," Joseph said, clearing his throat.

"It started with a cold," Belle said.

"But after he got over it, he came down with another one and then another one after that. Michael's working on his PhD and Sofia's working at the TV station, so neither of them could take a whole lot of time off, and Jay couldn't go to daycare when he kept getting sick," Joseph continued. "Then, last week, Michael noticed Jay's abdomen was swollen and took him to the ER. They did a bunch of tests . . ."

"Leukemia," Belle said tightly. "Acute lymphocytic leukemia."

"I'm so sorry!" Nicole exclaimed.

"That is absolutely heart wrenching," Josh said, thinking of how he'd feel if one of his own boys were given such a diagnosis. It was unimaginable. "I'm so sorry."

Belle blinked away sudden tears. "Well, the doctors are very optimistic. Apparently, this type of cancer—it's called ALL for short—is very common, especially in little guys."

"And it has a very high recovery rate," Joseph added. "Treatment for ALL can take several years. However, when it's treated successfully, it usually never comes back."

"That's good news. But it still must be so terrifying to have a little one go through that," Nicole said. The room was silent as Nicole thought about her son Gavin, who was not much older than Jay. She couldn't imagine—didn't want too, really—her child being sick like Jay. The idea was just too painful. Josh's sons were older, but he remembered all too well when his son came down with mono while on spring break—the tiredness, lack of appetite, lack of spirit. When the doctor dismissed cancer as a possibility, Josh's knees went weak—at the time, he hadn't even considered it as a possibility! Now, the thought of Joseph's grandson engulfed in such a tough health battle made Josh's own eyes damp.

"Enough of this!" Joseph said. "My grandson will be just fine. And this retirement . . . it's a good thing. It will give me what I want most. Time and freedom."

"What do you mean?" Nicole asked.

"I want time with my grandson. Not because he's going to die," Joseph added fiercely. "But because I want to be with him. His parents both need to work. Heaven knows Sofia can't give up her job—she's the one who has the medical coverage. And Michael can't just take off from his studies. But I can go down to Atlanta and be with my grandson. I can stay with him in the hospital during his first round of treatment, and I can be with him when he goes home, when his immunities are low and he can't be around other children. I will fix him his favorite mac and cheese and I will read him that book he always wants me to read over and over. Usually, I will read it two, maybe three times, and then I say, no, let's do something else. But this time, I'll say, 'Sure, buddy, as many times as you want.'"

Belle sniffed quietly. Nicole reached for the tissue box on the side table and passed it around to Belle.

"This is your doing, Josh Kadish," Joseph said, pointing his finger. Josh looked startled. "Mine? What do you mean?"

"You started with the questions, seven years ago. What was important to me, to Belle? What did retirement look like for us? Belle—remember that?"

"I do. When Joseph came home from that very first seminar with you, he asked me that question, too. It made us think, Josh," Belle said. "And then a few years later, we did the LifePrinting exercises you gave us, and that helped us think more concretely about life after work. That gave us an exit plan. It certainly helped Joseph be patient enough to wait on retirement, knowing that in the end, he would have more flexibility."

"We did that test drive on a retirement budget," Joseph recalled. "Remember you suggested we do that?" he asked Josh.

"Sure do," Josh said. "A lot of people who are anticipating retirement are surprised when they see what they can and cannot afford when they are actually living on a retirement budget. It can be very useful to try out that projected budget for six months or so before retiring and see if it is feasible for a lifetime."

"It was a challenge," Joseph said. "We tried it for four months and found that we could pay the essential bills, but we didn't have very much left over for enjoyment."

"As for me," Belle added, "that test drive made me realize that if I could contribute during those eight years, even on a part-time basis, it would add to the pot. I started working again, first part-time, then full-time as a bookkeeper for a law firm. I could see how my earnings would improve our retirement options. I'll be working with them through this next tax-filing season, when Joseph will be in Atlanta. Then, in about six months or so, if Jay is better—*when* Jay is better—we can decide what we want to do with the rest of our retirement."

"It's funny. When I initially thought about retirement, the first thing I thought of was the glory of being done with my job," Joseph said. "Being done with the headaches of micromanagement and bosses who change their agendas and goals as frequently as they change their socks. Done with the stress of production schedules and all of that. I was thinking about what I *didn't* want. But then, with you, Josh, and you, Nicole, I started thinking about what I *did* want. But even then, it was the stereotypical idea of retirement. Live in The Villages down in Florida and play golf every day. Ha! I've never played golf in my life, but that was what I thought retirement was supposed to be.

"But when Jay got sick, it hit me. If given the chance, I want to be with him. Even before I got the retirement package, even before Michael and Sofia knew for sure what was wrong, I started going down there on weekends, just to be with him. It's not just for me. I want him to know his Papa. Just like he got sick, I could get sick."

"Joseph! Don't say that!" Belle said sharply.

"It's true. We're not guaranteed a damned thing. When Jay got sick, I realized that my idea—our idea—of retirement didn't need to be what anybody else thought. If, after Jay's treatment, we want to sell our house and buy an RV and travel across the country like nomads, so what?"

"I'm not riding across the country in an RV!" Belle exclaimed.

"That was just an example," Joseph said, patting his wife's hand. "My point is, we get to define our own version of retirement, and because we've been preparing financially by being reasonably frugal and by making smart investments, when this came along—Jay's illness and the retirement offer—we have the freedom to do what we want."

"That is what we strive for," Josh said. "The things you mentioned, time and freedom—those aren't things money can buy, but when you plan your finances carefully, you get those options. And they're particularly important when life doesn't go as expected."

"Joseph, when will you be leaving for Atlanta?" Nicole asked.

"Tomorrow. I had planned to use my vacation days for the trip even before we got the package, so that will take care of several weeks. Then

I was planning to come back and officially take the retirement offer."

"All right," Josh said, "let's do this: we'll review the details of the package and plug the numbers into your financial analysis to see how this impacts your overall plan. We can also take a look at the next six months and determine what your budget should be. Then, once Jay is better and tax season is over, you and Belle can begin thinking of your next phase, of what scenarios you might see. Since you'll be gone, Joseph, let's set up a WebEx Internet meeting to go over them and see if you have any questions."

"That's a good plan," Joseph said, standing up. As Josh extended his hand, Joseph clasped Josh's hand between both of his. "Thank you."

Nicole went straight for the hug with both Belle and Joseph. "Let us know how Jay is doing."

"We will," Joseph promised as the couple left the office.

❂ ❂ ❂ Seven months later, Josh and Nicole greeted Joseph and Belle in the conference room once again.

"How's Jay doing?" Nicole asked immediately.

"He's doing very well," Joseph nodded with satisfaction. "Surpassing the doctors' expectations. He's finished the round of chemotherapy and is starting to get his energy back. I'm actually just here for the weekend, helping Belle wrap up some things, but then I'm heading back."

"How long will you be down there?" Nicole asked.

"Well, that's what we wanted to talk with you about," Joseph said as he looked at Belle. "We want to sell our house and move to Atlanta to be near our son and watch our grandson grow up."

"Sofia and Michael asked us to move in with them," Belle said. "And we may do that for a few months, but we need to find our own place. We love our family, but I can't imagine three generations of Silvas together under one roof," she laughed.

"So we'll find our own place nearby," Joseph explained. "But even though we're selling our house here, we don't want to buy—we want to rent, at least for now."

"But someplace nice," Belle interjected. "We want to travel, visit friends, go on a cruise, but have a home base to return to."

"Maybe we should get an RV," Joseph suggested slyly.

"No RV," Belle replied, as Joseph chuckled.

Joseph and Belle made a great pair, Nicole thought as she watched the couple's interplay. They communicated with each other, supported each other, and had a great sense of humor.

"We'll still have to be careful with money, I know," Joseph said. "Retiring at sixty-two still leaves a lot of time."

"True," Nicole said. "But because you've been budget-conscious these last few years, you didn't have to experience a huge monthly budget decrease after your retirement. We also ran a Social Security optimization analysis for you and determined that the right claiming strategy may provide an additional $240,000 in benefits, which can help ensure you can maintain your standard of living throughout retirement."

"Yes. Even after we finished that retirement test drive, we tried to stick somewhat closer to that budget—with some leeway now and then. It certainly helped. But wow! I had no idea that even something like claiming Social Security could be so complicated. I thought it was simple: take benefits at sixty-two, sixty-six, or seventy. That's it!" Joseph said. "I thought, okay, I'm retiring now so start taking the benefits while there is still money in the Social Security system before it goes broke."

"You two are in a very good position," Josh agreed. "You may tweak your ideas of what retirement looks like—whether you rent now and buy later, and how to stay within your budget while still having flexibility to travel. But your preparation, the hard work you started years ago, put you in this position. Now that we found an extra couple hundred thousand dollars from Social Security," Josh said with a smile, "let's take a look at how selling your house here and renting in Atlanta affects your financial plan."

Joseph laid a hand on Josh's arm, stilling him.

"Thank you. When I first came to you, years ago, I didn't envision this. I didn't know I'd be honored to have the chance to spend this time with my grandson and that I would be able to act upon it. Suppose I couldn't do that, because I didn't have the money? I'm sure Jay would have gotten better with or without me there, but I like to think that maybe I helped.

"But even more, it was a gift to me to be there. I found that 'True Wealth' that you talked about. My True Wealth is having the luxury to be with my family and having the finances that give me the flexibility to do it."

Josh smiled broadly. This was what he and Nicole lived for every day. Seeing a plan come together so that their clients could enjoy their lives. Helping them reach a higher level of awareness about what real happiness and success looked like for them. Helping people reevaluate their status quo to see if they are genuinely fulfilling their potential and then figuring out the best way to make it happen.

"Joseph, believe me, it's our pleasure. This is *our* purpose, and we are so pleased to help you make this work. Next on our agenda can be figuring out what your newfound gypsy life might look like!"

EARLY RETIREMENT: ADVICE FROM JOSH AND NICOLE

Through Joseph and Belle, we get to see an excellent example of a financial planning success story. Although Joseph had wanted to retire for years, he realized he was not prepared financially. But because he had anticipated retiring, he was ready to take advantage of it when the opportunity presented itself. The timing turned out to be exceptional, allowing him to be with his grandson. The preparation he had done years in advance gave him flexibility when life became uncertain.

We often recommend that people anticipating retirement do a "test drive" by living three to six months on their retirement budget. Can they do it comfortably? If not, it is much better to discover this while they are still employed. The test drive allows time to make changes to income, budgets, investment directions, or retirement dates. Belle decided that she could contribute to the family income so that they would benefit in the future, and that decision paid off.

Illness, whether one's own or that of a loved one, has an amazing way of clarifying goals and dreams. In addition to taking care of their grandson, Joseph and Belle also more clearly defined how they wanted to live out their retirement years, and solid planning gave them the opportunity to follow their dream.

LIFEPRINTING QUESTIONS

1. How do you envision your retirement?
   * Where you will live
   * Whether you will work full or part time

- Hobbies
- Travel

2. What is truly important to you?
   - Time with family
   - Health
   - Volunteering
   - Charity

3. How much will you need to live the life you envision?
   - What is the probability of success based on the assets you currently have?
   - How can you improve your probability of success?
     - Social Security optimization analysis
     - Tax-reduction strategies
     - Tax-efficient investing
     - Retirement test drive
     - Proper healthcare coverage
     - Review all current insurance coverage and determine if you still have a need for coverage

CHAPTER 11

THE DREAM WAS BETTER THAN REALITY
CLIENT STORY: B.J. CHAPMAN

"BE CAREFUL WHAT YOU WISH FOR . . ."
Anonymous

"It was great to finally meet you, Josh," said David Marx as he stood up from the table of the Allworth Financial conference room. "I'm very impressed with your organization, and I'm looking forward to having you work with our players." David clasped Josh's hand in a strong shake and, after saying goodbye, made his way toward the reception area.

Josh gathered his notes into a folder, smiling with satisfaction. An age-old dream was being realized. As avid sports fans, Josh and Nicole relished the opportunity to work with sports agents, business managers, and athlete clientele. So many kids dream of being professional athletes, scoring the last second game winner, being cheered by fans, and living the good life. But Josh and Nicole knew that too often, the real story ended much differently.

Allwroth Financial had finally made it to the big time! Securing a relationship with one of the top agents at a prominent sports agency took Allworth Financial into a whole other world—the world of the professional athlete; the glitz and the glamour of celebrities, sporting events, big contracts, big bonuses, and big business. For years, Josh had sat on the proverbial sidelines cheering for his favorite teams and play-ers. Now, the dream of having some of those players as clients of his firm was turning into reality.

Two weeks after his meeting with David Marx, Josh was hopping aboard a last-minute flight to Huntsville, Alabama, and then driving two hours to Starkville, Mississippi, to meet a future NBA prospect. An hour into the drive, from the airport to the university, Josh's cell phone rang.

"The kid's not going to make the meeting," said the voice on the other end of the line. It was one of David's assistants, already waiting at the hotel in Starkville and handling the business of this future star.

"Are you kidding me, Trey?" Josh said in stunned disbelief. "I've been traveling for four hours to get there and he's not showing up? What's going on?"

"His dad is with some chick and can't get here for the four p.m. meeting," Trey explained matter-of-factly.

Josh shook his head. "This is B.S., Trey. Get the kid to the meeting, even without his father. Let me get in front of him and at least meet him. It's the least they can do for having me drop everything to see him."

Trey must have done some convincing, because by the time Josh reached the hotel, the 6'9" twenty-one-year old "kid" was waiting for him.

"Hi, I'm Josh," he said with an outstretched hand. But even as Josh shook hands with the phenom, the twenty-one-year old was obviously ill at ease, giving a limp handshake in return and staring at the ground, avoiding eye contact. Josh had always been a people person, genuinely caring about helping those he met. He'd sat with thousands of people as he built his practice over the previous fourteen years. But as they sat in the hotel conference room, an uncomfortable tension descended. Despite Josh's efforts, there was no connection. The boy displayed no humor, no personality. The meeting seemed as if it was over before it even started. Josh would never see or talk to this kid again.

◎ ◎ ◎ "B.J. is projected to be top five in the draft in a few months," business manager Darryl Beaufort proudly proclaimed of his future NFL star. He had worked tirelessly for years to secure him.

"That's awesome," Josh responded. He was excited but kept his voice down. Although his meeting with the NBA prospect had fizzled, Josh remained hopeful and began working with other agents and business managers to the stars. It was nearly midnight, and he didn't want to wake his young sons, who were asleep down the hall. He and Tracy had just started to doze off, too, when his cell phone rang. Josh looked at the number, sat up, and quickly left the bedroom to take the call. Running down the stairs, he now stood in the middle of his boys' playroom—the first room he reached where he could close the door so his voice wouldn't travel.

"You guys can assume that we'll invest about twenty-five percent of the signing bonus with you and then more once B.J. buys the things he wants out of the gate," Darryl continued.

"Three to five years. That's the average career of a professional athlete," Josh had told Nicole two months earlier as they prepared a proposal for Darryl Beaufort detailing services they could provide to B.J. Josh had worked for a year to network with agents, and after a lot of hard work, he had been introduced to Darryl.

"And in that time, they can earn millions of dollars," Nicole said. "But in the same amount of time or less, it can all be gone."

Josh nodded. Although a professional athlete could earn more in just three years than the average person could in a twenty- to thirty-year career, many of those same players went bankrupt as soon as their professional career ended. It was such a shame, Josh thought. And it wasn't necessarily the kids' fault. The sad truth was that those kids were boosted to a level of stardom before they even hit the big time. Scouted and courted by coaches as early as junior high school, the kids were enticed to play for a particular high school. Then they were courted to select a specific college. Once they were enrolled, the coddling didn't stop. From special help with classes to overly lenient professors, many star athletes had people doing almost everything for them. It was no surprise, then, that by the time many of these kids went pro, they had developed an attitude of indulgence, privilege, and excess. The vast majority of these talented kids and their families had no real business savvy or experience handling money. Fame and fortune lured them and, unfortunately, the friends and family around them as well.

So when the opportunity came to work with standout college junior B.J. Chapman, the Allworth Financial team was excited. Unlike Nicole and Josh's typical clients, B.J. didn't have an income yet, but he was expected to be offered a multimillion-dollar signing bonus and contract when he was drafted in the spring. Josh hoped to have the chance to talk with B.J. in person soon. Since all of his interactions so far had been with the business manager, it was difficult to get a read on the star athlete or on what he might be thinking about his personal and financial future.

"We've been watching his games as well as the draft boards, and we're excited to work with you and B.J.!" Josh said to Darryl, as he leaned down and picked up a plastic video game case from the floor. He set the case down on the Xbox console. His boys had so much—toys, games, a beautiful house, and a loving family. Josh often wondered if his kids appreciated what they had.

"Great." Darryl's rumbling voice caught Josh's attention. "So, here's the deal. B.J. wants a black Mercedes S600."

Josh nearly laughed, before realizing Darryl wasn't joking. *Are you kidding me? He's all of what, twenty years old?* But Josh's professional side prevailed.

"Okay, well, when he's drafted in about twelve weeks, we'll introduce him to our contacts at Mercedes and get it all worked out," he said smoothly.

"B.J. wants the car now. Let us know what you can do," Darryl replied. He still sounded congenial, but Josh could hear the hint of testiness underlying his tone.

"Darryl, come on." Josh combed his fingers through his hair in frustration. "If you're his business manager and I'm his wealth manager, we have a responsibility to look out for his best interests. There's no way that getting this kid a $160,000 car before he graduates or is even drafted is in his best interest. Surely you know that."

"It's what the kid wants, and part of working with him is helping him get what he wants, right?" Darryl pressed. Josh could tell he was being tested, but why? Weren't he and Darryl supposed to be a team, both looking out for B.J.?

"That's just not going to happen," Josh said. "Someone has to tell B.J. no. Do you ever try that?"

"Josh, you're new at working with athletes. I've been doing this for a while now. And it's a game. You get them what they want, and everyone is happy. And if you don't get them what they want, they'll find someone else who can. So come on," Darryl cajoled. "Let's be happy."

"So we'll all spend our time trying to locate a car, which is nearly impossible to find, and then have to get the money for him with no credit, no contract, and no collateral," Josh said, sure that when he summarized it, Darryl would also see how ridiculous it was.

"That's right," Darryl said.

Josh sighed. Maybe he'd do this one thing, reassure Darryl that he was able to pull out a win, gain B.J.'s trust, get him on board, and then Josh could begin to actually help him make solid financial plans.

"Okay, I'm on it," Josh finally agreed. "But it will likely be a thirty percent interest rate to borrow money, and that will be done without me directly involved."

"Thanks, buddy!" Darryl said. "I know you'll make it happen. Don't forget we also have the top major league baseball prospect coming your way, so all your hard work will pay off!"

And that was the teaser. The promise of more relationships. As Josh hung up the phone, he stood there, wondering, as he had often in the past few months, was it worth it? Were he and Nicole just adrenaline junkies, thrilled by the chase, excited by the idea of working with such a different clientele?

Ever since he and Nicole first considered actively recruiting athletes as a segment of their clientele, it was obvious that life at that level was different. Of course, many of their potential clients in the NBA and NFL had more money than the typical corporate executive. The athletes were usually much younger—twenty, thirty, even forty years younger. They hadn't experienced many of life's ups and downs. They thought they would always be in the spotlight; that fans would always clamor for them; that their achievements—or exploits—would always be big news. Most of them hadn't experienced the heartbreak of the loss of a loved one, a serious illness, or the loss of a job. And although these facts made it more challenging for young athletes to understand why they should work on a lifelong financial plan, it also made Josh and Nicole even more determined to help them understand—and prepare.

"Josh? What are you doing?" Tracy opened the door to the playroom. "On the phone again?"

Josh nodded. "It was Darryl. I had to take it."

"Is everything okay?" she asked.

Josh nodded. "This kid wants a Mercedes S600."

"You're kidding, right?" she asked.

Josh shrugged.

"Oh, honey, that's just crazy. This whole thing is crazy, isn't it? I mean, I know and love what you and Nicole are trying to do, but it's putting such a strain on you. Look at what's happening right now. It's after midnight on a Sunday night, and you're on the phone. Besides that, you're at these guys' beck and call, jumping on planes to the middle of nowhere to meet this kid that's gonna be great or that kid who's being drafted early."

Tracy put a reassuring hand on Josh's arm, her dark eyes concerned. "You know I support whatever you do, but this is starting to take its toll on you and on us. We don't have family time like we used to. You missed the boys' basketball games last week to run off to meet another kid who wasn't even interested in what you could offer him. And you don't seem like you're enjoying it. You're doing all this, and it's just to *get* one of these clients. Will it be even worse once you actually have one?"

Josh couldn't help but bristle at the question, even gently worded. But then he relaxed. He didn't need to be defensive with Tracy. She had always been his biggest cheerleader and had a clarity that cut through all of the stuff he had been dealing with lately. It was possible—probable, even—that she had a point.

⊘ ⊘ ⊘ "Remind me, Nicole, why did we decide this was a good idea?" Josh asked half kiddingly as he ended a phone call. Black Mercedes S600s were difficult to find.

"It was a good idea," Nicole said. "When we did our own LifePrinting exercises, we discussed what our own passions were. One of yours is sports. It's something you've always wanted to explore, and you have."

"Yeah. And look where it's gotten us. No closer than we were before. And what I've seen of the business, I don't really like," Josh said. "This is not what I envisioned when I thought about it. My passion isn't for hopping on airplanes and kowtowing to people who don't care about preparing for their future. I want to help educate them, help them have security in their future."

Nicole gave a small laugh.

"What's so funny?" Josh asked, a little hurt. He had been sincere.

"I'm not laughing at you. Well, maybe I'm laughing a little at both of us," Nicole said. "What you said about this not being what you envisioned. That sounds so much like both of us when we started out in the business. We both knew what we wanted to do, what we could accomplish, the positive impact we could make—we just couldn't find the right place to do it."

Josh remembered his first meeting with Nicole, when she said how important it was to educate and provide her clients with tools so they could make good decisions.

"You're kind of saying the same thing," Nicole continued. "There's nothing wrong with your passion—you just have to focus it on the people who will appreciate it."

Josh thought about that for a moment. "So what you're saying is we need to find athletes who want to learn and maybe stop chasing the ones who are still so young and haven't experienced a life transition that makes them realize how important it is to get good advice."

"Ding-ding," Nicole said playfully.

Josh had a fleeting memory of that long-ago day in the hotel in Boston, when he sat on the bed in misery, realizing that the highly coveted job wasn't right for him. Perhaps the same was happening here: chasing after celebrity athletes brought that adrenaline high, but it sure didn't sustain it.

This was what he and Nicole talked about with clients all the time, he realized. What mattered? What was important? There was nothing wrong with pursuing new ideas, but he also had to take a moment and evaluate them to see if their reality still matched his core values, his passion.

But for now, there was still the question of B.J., the potential client. Josh and Nicole agreed to keep trying to work with him while they refined who their true athlete client should be. Like hunting a near-extinct white rhino, Josh and his team located and secured the elusive black-on-black S600, and the mission was accomplished. Everyone was happy . . . for three months.

"Uh, Josh?" Josh had never heard Darryl sound so uncertain before.

"Hey, Darryl, how's our guy?" Josh asked.

"Well, he got hurt today in practice. Looks like it's his knee."

That NFL scouting combine, which occurred every February, was just weeks away.

"Will he recover in time?" Josh asked, already knowing the answer. He shook his head, although Darryl couldn't see him. This. This was what he had warned them about. Every player is one play away from being retired! Sure, B.J. had his Mercedes, but now perhaps nothing to show for his promise except an enormous car loan.

Sure enough, in the weeks leading up to the combine, B.J.'s injury was slow to heal. Unable to participate in the combine, the potential top draft pick ended up with one of the biggest drops in the draft, falling to the second round with no signing bonus and no rich contract.

"I didn't want this, not even to be proven right," Josh said to Nicole the day after the draft.

"Neither of us did. But this also teaches us a lesson. We need to identify the people, whether they're retirees or widows or young couples or athletes, who value what we can provide and who want to learn," Nicole said. "We have to keep refining our business model to make sure it supports our passion, who we really are, and what we want to do. We'll keep our eyes open for those folks who really fit what we want."

"You're right," Josh admitted.

"As always," Nicole laughed.

❂ ❂ ❂ A few months later, Nicole knocked on Josh's door. "A good friend from my childhood has a brother who was just signed to the Seattle Seahawks practice squad. I ran into his parents yesterday, and they're interested in me talking to him. This is one kid that I know came from a good family. He's smart and savvy. His agent is a good guy who likes the idea of helping him plan his financial future."

Josh grinned. This sounded more like it. As Nicole sat down across from Josh and the two discussed details, they felt a warm surge of promise that came with knowledge that they were moving in the right direction.

NEW WEALTH: NOTES FROM JOSH AND NICOLE

Ahh. To win the lottery. Or to be an athlete, entertainer, or entrepreneur and suddenly have people offering you more money than you've ever seen before. It's tempting. And for so many young phenoms, the glory—and the money—can be fleeting. When a person gets a windfall, such as through a major sports contract, almost everyone wants a cut—deservedly or not. Sound financial planning makes it easier to determine thoughtful ways to handle those requests and to invest the money. Many young upstarts are so used to hearing yes to their every wish that it takes someone who is intent on looking out for their best interest to sometimes say no, or "I don't think that's the best course." It may not be what the client initially wants to hear, but it is what the client *should* hear. For people like "the kid" at the beginning of this story and B.J. at the end, a thorough understanding of finances—and a team with which to review them as circumstances change—helps protect their money . . . and their future.

It's important to have good people around you. Realize that those people are not necessarily the ones who give you everything you want or agree with everything that you say.

It's important to be realistic as to how long any career may last. Statistically speaking, the average career of a professional athlete is fewer than five years. Plan for that and if you last longer, then your plan will look better.

Think about what you might like to do after your playing days are over. You can lay the foundation for that eventuality even when you are playing. Your image is everything so make sure you focus on that as well as being the best player you can be. If you have a reputation for being a well-spoken, responsible, and caring person while you are playing, that will pay off big time in the opportunities that may be available later in life. Michael Jordan may have been one of the best athletes of all time but Nike, Gatorade, and a host of other corporations paid him hundreds of millions of dollars because he had a sterling reputation and was always viewed as a good guy.

You're never too young to start planning for your future. Be sure to take the time to find holistic advisors that are held to a fiduciary standard where they are required to do what is in your best interest. And finally, always follow your gut feeling on those people around you. You're probably right.

QUESTIONS TO ASK POTENTIAL ADVISORS

1. How long have you been doing this?
2. How many clients do you have like me?
3. How do you get paid?

   If they earn commissions, realize they may be tempted to invest your money for their own benefit, not yours.
4. Are you held to a fiduciary standard?

   If they are a fiduciary, it is the highest standard available and they are required to do what is in your best interest. This is different than the majority of advisors that are only held to a suitability standard. **Beware: just because they are supposed to be held to a fiduciary standard doesn't mean they will live up to it.**
5. What services do you provide?

   Don't expect an insurance agent to advise you on investments and vice versa. Don't expect that an accountant does anything more than accounting, and so on.
6. Will you be my one-stop resource for investments, insurance, and tax and estate planning?
7. How many people are on your staff to support me?
8. Will I be working directly with you or someone else?
9. What happens if you are no longer here?
10. What is your succession plan?
11. Where are my assets held and how are checks to be made payable when I want to add to my accounts?

    No checks should ever be made payable to an individual or their "company name" where they will sweep to an account for you. All checks should be payable to larger institutions after accounts have been opened in your own name or your own trust.
12. Aside from running numbers, how do you identify what is important to me?
13. How often will we meet?
14. How will we meet?

    Telephone, in-person, internet?

15. Are you fully transparent on all fees?

This answer must be "YES!" and they should provide a fee schedule.

16. Do you share any compensation with any other relationship you may introduce me to?

17. Are you independent?

Advisors that are independent typically have more flexibility to shop for solutions for you since they aren't required to only promote a single company.

AFTERWORD

In September 2013, as I (Josh) lay in a hospital bed, I thought about this book and the advice we wanted to impart to readers. My experience in the hospital, undergoing treatment for kidney stones, illustrated once again the emotions that many of our clients experience as well. I'm used to being in control of almost all situations; yet, there I was, with absolutely no control, nervous and anxious about what was to come. I was dependent on the "experts" to advise and treat me. Despite various doctors and nurses giving me advice and telling me what they were going to do, what was palpably missing from our conversations was true communication. These experts talked *at* me, not *with* me. One didn't know what the other one said, which made a stressful situation that much worse. If someone had stopped and taken a moment to explain to me and all others involved what was going on and why, made sure we all understood, and then helped me understand the next steps and available options, I certainly would have been far more at ease in a frightening and painful situation.

This is a powerful parallel to the services we provide to our clients as they undergo their own life transitions. It is essential to take a step back and listen to the concerns of our client, to ensure they understand the situation—and educate them if they do not—in order to help them determine the option that enables them to proceed with more confidence and less anxiety and uncertainty. Whether a person is starting a lucrative career, in between jobs, going through a divorce, facing an illness, taking care of an aging relative, entering retirement, mourning the loss of a loved one, or simply seeking a second opinion, it's an unsettling time, and our role is to be a source of education, information, and expertise.

Nearly twenty years ago, I (Josh) was told to just write the damned ticket—selling investments to someone whether they truly met that person's need or not. Even then, it was clear that the financial industry was broken. It wasn't structured to actually help clients meet their long-term financial goals; it was structured to help companies meet their quotas and grow their bottom line.

You would think that would have changed over time. Yet, almost fifteen years later, as a newcomer in the business, I (Nicole) was admonished to sell a client a product that did not take into account her individual concerns, goals, or needs.

Allworth Financials' focus on education and customized, strategic long-term planning still makes us a pioneer in the industry. Our practice of ensuring that clients have the knowledge and confidence to make a good decision is still unique. But we subscribe to the adage of teaching a man to fish, not just fishing for him, and certainly not trying to sell the fish to him.

Some financial planners have incorporated an educational compo-nent to their offering but still do not use a holistic approach. Without taking into consideration your core values, what is truly important to you, and whether your financial and personal actions support that, how can someone advise you on how to prepare properly for your future?

In our careers, we have both had many of the same transitions as our clients. Changing career paths, getting married, expanding our families, coping with divorce, and caring for aging relatives—we can relate to our clients. We recognize that each client's situation is unique, but we can draw on our own experiences for a deeper understanding of the emo-tions that they may be feeling. We understand that it takes much more than money or a specific product to bring them happiness and, ultimately, financial freedom.

To maintain our deep commitment to client privacy, their names and some details were changed. Although many of the clients who inspired the stories in this book live in the Chicago area, near our offices, thanks to the benefits of technology, our clients do not need to be within shout-ing distance of us. We have clients all around the world, and with email, web conferencing, and the old-fashioned telephone, we create a strong relationship with them no matter where they are.

Whether you wish to contact us or seek someone else to advise you on your current course, it is essential to ask some tough questions at the start.

1. Are your potential advisors asking the right questions? Are they asking you purely about your financial direction, or are they interested in getting to know your concerns, your unique circumstances, and your vision—in other words, *you*?

2. Are they explaining what they do? How much is education a part of their process? Even if you don't need a certain aspect explained, are they checking to confirm that?

3. Do they offer a review of your current progress, or do they just tell you what you should do differently?

4. Are they advising or selling? When the conversation turns quickly to the product to buy, the focus is no longer on what's best for you, but on what is best for them.

5. Are they suggesting you take the appropriate amount of risk? Some planners seduce clients with promises of quick results, but this usually comes with unacceptable levels of risk. Does the suggested direction provide enough security for your long-term goals?

6. Did they give you a plan? Have they discussed the importance of proper Social Security claiming strategies? A plan is long term, taking into consideration your retirement vision and lifestyle, and is developed to ensure you can reach those goals. Some "financial planners" provide direction but never actually get you to the end point.

7. Are they genuine? Do you feel that you are appreciated and attended to? Are your questions answered thoroughly and respectfully? Do they demonstrate that they appreciate your time and trust? Are they communicating well with you?

Yes, the financial industry is broken, but in some areas, repairs are being made. Companies are beginning to understand the benefits of the holistic, client-centered approach. But you have to look for them. Look for the select few who are held to a fiduciary standard. You have to ask tough questions. You have to have high expectations and ensure they are met. Now that you know the importance of comprehensive planning, we en-courage you to seek out Allworth Financial and firms like us that are committed to helping you navigate life's transitions, connect your means to your meaning, and ultimately, find your *True Wealth*.

ABOUT JOSH KADISH, AIF, BFA, RFC

Josh graduated from the University of Wisconsin-Madison with a double major in international relations and political science, before going on to become a founding partner at 2nd Opinion Partners now know as Allworth Financial. He was called to cre-ate the company after realizing many financial services were not offering heart-first, personalized financial advice for clients.

Throughout his career, Josh has garnered recognition. He has been an author, visionary, and mentor at 2nd Opinion Partners. His expertise has been featured in the *Wall Street Journal*, *Money* magazine, *Kiplinger's Personal Finance*, and other major publications. He is an NFLPA Regis-tered Player Financial Advisor, Accredited Investment Fiduciary (AIF), Behavioral Financial Advisor (BFA), and Registered Financial Consultant (RFC). He holds FINRA Series 7, 63, and 65 licenses. With Nicole Mayer he cowrote *Navigating Life's Transitions: Connecting Your Means to Your Meaning*, which became an Amazon Top Seller.

Josh's true calling, however, has always been to make a positive im-pact on other lives. When he looks back, he remembers with pride the birth of his two sons, trips to Abacos, Bahamas, and attending a 2016 Cubs World Series game with his sons, father, and father-in-law. He re-members the time spent with his grandmother and mother and the times he attended Senior Spring Break trips with his sons, as well as his trip to pay respects at the 9/11 Memorial and Ground Zero.

Josh wants everyone to experience moments that mean this much to them, and he knows that money is part of the equation (and only a part of it). This realization has made him fully committed to helping his clients and readers lead lives of prosperity and sound financial decision-making.

ABOUT NICOLE MAYER, AIF, BFA, CDFA, RFC

As a founding partner at 2nd Opinion Partners now know as Allworth Financial, an author, and a speaker, Nicole has a passion for educating clients and helping them celebrate their big financial wins. She also honors the times when clients turn to her at their most vulnerable moments.

At Allworth Financial Nicole mentors new team members, supports client experience development, and works directly with clients. Outside the firm, she has been featured on Fox Business News, WGN Channel 9 News, and CNBC. Her book *Navigating Life's Transitions: Con-necting Your Means to Your Meaning*, cowritten with Joshua Kadish, was an Amazon Top Seller.

Nicole graduated from DePaul University with a major in finance and marketing. She is an Accredited Investment Fiduciary (AIF), Behavioral Financial Advisor (BFA), Certified Divorce Financial Analyst (CDFA), and Registered Financial Consultant (RFC). She holds FINRA Series 7 and 66 licenses.

Nicole treasures memories such as the birth of her son, her college graduation, and her first home purchase. She treasures the long days she and her team put in to found the company that would become 2nd Opinion Partners now known as Allworth Financial.

Nicole's professional and personal experience has deepened her desire to help people and to offer better educational tools they can use to transform their lives.

DISCLAIMERS

◉ ◉ ◉ Financial planning is challenging. It becomes more challenging as you begin to factor in such things as individual wants and desires. This is compounded by variables such as unique personal circumstances and ever-changing regulations. This book reflects the authors' opinions. These opinions are not intended to provide specific advice and should not be construed as recommendations for any individual. This book is published with the understanding that the authors are not engaged in rendering legal or tax services. Investments involve risk including potential for loss of the principal amount invested. Past performance is no guarantee of future results. Please remember that investment decisions should be based on an individual's goals, time horizon, and tolerance for risk. The services of competent legal, tax, and financial professionals should be sought prior to executing any strategy. The characters and stories in this book are a dramatization of actual events. Names, circumstances, and advice are a compilation of several clients we have encountered over the years. No one story is based on a particular client.